THE LIFE STORY OF AN
ESSEX BOY

THE LIFE STORY OF AN
ESSEX BOY

ERIC HOBBS

Matador
9 Priory Business Park,
Wistow Road, Kibworth Beauchamp,
Leicestershire. LE8 0RX
Tel: (+44) 116 279 2299
Fax: (+44) 116 279 2277
Email: books@troubador.co.uk
Web: www.troubador.co.uk/matador

ISBN 978 1783061 389

British Library Cataloguing in Publication Data.
A catalogue record for this book is available from the British Library.

Typeset by Troubador Publishing Ltd, Leicester, UK

Matador is an imprint of Troubador Publishing Ltd

I dedicate this book to all the people who I have not mentioned by name but who have helped me on my way through life.

Looking back to remember times gone by has been a fascinating process. Having sifted through my memory banks, trawled through old photograph albums, and shared memories around the table, the final result is this book, which I hope will not only be of interest but will also help to raise funds for the Essex Air Ambulance. I am extremely grateful for Margaret's input in both recalling and writing our story, and I am also grateful to Jo Roberts from JMD Editorial and Writing Services, 01376 554844, who has been invaluable in correcting my spelling and bad grammar.

If you know others that would be interested in reading this book, rather than loaning it to friends or colleagues, please encourage them to purchase a copy from Essex Air Ambulance, and help support this deserving charity:

The Essex Air Ambulance
The Business Centre
Earls Colne Business Park,
Earls Colne
Colchester
Essex
C06 2NS

£10.00 plus P&P

Essex Air Ambulance is a Helicopter Emergency Medical Service (HEMS); providing a free life-saving service for Essex and surrounding areas, specialist doctors and critical care paramedics can be rushed to the scene of an incident with life-saving support equipment, and the patient, following assessment, will be flown to the most appropriate hospital.

Unlike NHS emergency services Essex Air Ambulance is a charity, relying solely upon the generosity and goodwill of the people and businesses of Essex to remain operational and saving lives, with their main sponsor being Wilkin & Sons.

The Essex Air Ambulance charity was established and began fundraising in 1997 with the first Air Ambulance being launched in July 1998 from New Hall School in Boreham. As the charity began to grow, the fundraising staff rapidly grew out of their office at Ambulance HQ in Broomfield, and in May 2004, following talks with E Hobbs Farms, the charity office moved to Earls Colne Business Park, providing the team with much improved office facilities and more spacious surroundings.

Nearly ten years later, the charity still occupies the very same offices, however, during this time the operation has continued to grow and develop as has the relationship with E Hobbs Farms. In April 2007 the Essex Air Ambulance charity became Essex & Herts Air Ambulance Trust (EHAAT) and is now responsible for operating two helicopters covering Essex and Hertfordshire. Following a big fundraising push the first Air Ambulance in Hertfordshire was launched by the Trust on 5th November 2008 and at the same time doctors were introduced to the air crew to work alongside specially trained paramedics from the ambulance service, providing the opportunity to take the hospital to the roadside.

Following three years of hard work and research to find the most suitable location to co-locate the Essex Air Base and Charity Office, in April 2011 the Essex Air Ambulance service relocated from Boreham to Earls Colne Airfield. As part of the relocation and with funding from ICAP, who made it all possible, a new visitor centre was created and opened in July 2011. For the first time the operation and the charity team could work side by side, bringing the life-saving helicopter closer to its supporters as well as offering a new facility to the community; special thanks must go to Michael Spencer of ICAP for his generosity.

Essex Air Ambulance is extremely grateful to Eric Hobbs for kindly donating all proceeds of this book to our life-saving charity, and to the people of Essex for their on-going support. With no direct government or National Lottery funding the charity is reliant upon donations from the public and local businesses to keep flying.

*The Essex Air Ambulance Visitor Centre at Earls Colne Business Park;
with special thanks to ICAP who funded the new building*

Essex and Herts Air Ambulance Trust staff and volunteers

Chapter 1 – How it All Began

Sitting here now, looking back at my life, it's hard to believe that I came from such humble beginnings, it's hard to believe that with no expectations placed upon me, I've strived and struggled to reach where I am today. It hasn't been an easy path to tread, but then of course, nothing worth having ever is; but on the whole it's been an exciting journey. I've relied a lot on hard work, on taking risks and on following my instinct; and I've relied an awful lot on luck, which has shined down on me and my family in the most extraordinary ways. I feel immensely grateful for the life I lead and for the unfailing support of the woman that's been by my side for over fifty years; I say by my side, but in all honesty she's been the one either pushing me along to follow my dreams, or pulling me along in order to keep up with her ideas and ambition. Between us we have raised a wonderful family who we both feel immensely proud of and I hope that this book will give them some knowledge about how it all came to be.

So, I suppose I should start with how it all began, which was with my mother, Joan Scott. She was a hard working young girl, employed in service in a large house in Herongate, Essex. Her parents, my grandparents, lived just two miles from her place of work, but despite this she was only ever allowed home to see them on Sunday afternoons. The rest of her week was spent toiling in the house, rising early to make fires to ensure that each of the rooms were suitably warm before the rest of the household awoke. Then she'd busy herself in the kitchen, scrubbing and peeling potatoes, slaving over cooking pots and doing whatever she could to ensure the house ran smoothly. It's fair to say she wasn't afraid of hard work, or of putting herself out there to undertake the mundane or potentially degrading jobs that came from being in service. Her life was seemingly consumed by work; every second of every day accounted for by either chores or sleeping in order to be ready to do it all again the following day. It still surprises me to this day then that she managed to find the time to meet my father, Walter Hobbs. He was a milkman who lived at Park Farm, a dairy farm in Dunton, a small parish next to the village of Herongate. His home was a simple two up, two down cottage, as most of the local residents were accustomed to. And every morning he'd rise before the rest of the village and start his day delivering milk to the population of Dunton and the other surrounding villages. He met my mother, I assume, on his rounds, no doubt clandestinely because she was seldom free to leave the house; but despite this, somehow they managed to meet, become acquainted, begin a courtship and eventually fall in love. And in 1934 the milkman and the housemaid married, and husband and wife moved into the two up, two down cottage to begin their married life together.

It wasn't long before Joan fell pregnant, and the following year, on the 16th of January 1935, their first child was born to them, that was me, Eric Hobbs. Soon after my birth our little family of three grew to a family of four, with the arrival of my sister Sheila, born in December 1935, less than a year after me. Looking back now I realise it must have been quite a squeeze to have all four of us living in that tiny cottage, but as a child you generally just accept that that's how things are, you don't question your surroundings or feel hard done by, especially not back then. And my parents, I suspect felt much the same; there wasn't such a yearning for material things as there is today, people weren't striving to prosper with such vigour as they are today, back then the majority were happy to lead the simple life, and that's exactly what we did.

We all plodded along nicely as we were, my father still working his rounds as a milkman and my mother content raising her two young children. But in 1939 everything changed. It was the start of the war and the end of our simple family life as we knew it. Our world was turned upside down when my father was called up to fight, as were all men of a certain age. My father was a fit young man who didn't hesitate to step up and do what was asked of him; he initially joined up as a rifleman in a rifle regiment, but after two years of service with them he volunteered to go into the parachute regiment. I'd like to say that he made the switch because he wanted to experience new adventures, or because he had a yearning to fly, but probably the real reason was purely because the money was better… it drives most of us in the end.

Chapter 2 – A Taste of Things to Come

With my father away with the army, my mother decided that it would be best if the rest of us went to live with my grandparents in their small bungalow in Herongate. I didn't mind living there one bit, in fact I loved it. My grandfather had a five acre smallholding, which he rented from the big estate where he worked. He started his employment there initially as a gardener, and then for many years he worked as a groom, and I believe that's where my love of horses originates from. The smallholding was indeed small, but at the time, as an innocent and rather naïve four year old I thought it was a massive estate by all accounts, and I loved helping my grandfather to work the land. I spent many happy days out in the field and living cosily inside the tiny two bedroom bungalow sited there.

My grandparents; I owe them so much

Whilst we were living there my second sister, Marie, was born in 1943, after my father had returned home briefly for leave nine months previously. And so, with the arrival of Marie it meant that I and my mother *and* my two sisters, all shared one room; but again, we never minded, we simply weren't concerned with things like that back then. We were just grateful that we had a roof over our heads, and a bed to sleep in, even if it was shared with three other people.

My grandfather had been renting the plot of land we were living on since 1930, renting for a very reasonable sum of thirty five pounds a year. And he continued to rent the plot until 1961, with the rent that he paid not being increased at all throughout the whole tenancy, making it an even more reasonable fee as the years went on. However, as the war progressed times started to change, previously affluent households were starting to struggle, and the poorer families had to tighten their belts even further, us included. The house that my grandfather worked at could no longer afford to employ him, but thankfully they were still happy and able to let him rent the bungalow and the land on which we were living. He made the most of the opportunities that the land provided; he kept two cows, had five or six pig stys, and a flock of two hundred chickens, which was particularly impressive considering that most people at the time only kept about two or three chickens in their back garden. All of my grandfather's livestock and hard work helped to provide us with food without eating into our allocated rations. He also grew soft fruit; strawberries and raspberries, only small plots of each, but a crop all the same. Whilst I was living there I learned a lot about livestock and the growing of soft fruit, and I truly believed I lived on a massive farm; it wasn't until later in life that I realised just how small my grandfather's smallholding was, a far cry from the vast farming empire I imagined it to be. But his 'empire' impressed me regardless, and my initial insight into his farming stayed with me eternally, and it inspired me to want to be a farmer too.

The border of my grandfather's land adjoined Thorndon

Park, just outside Brentwood, and at the time the war agricultural committee had powers to instruct landowners to either plough up their land or let others graze it with cattle or sheep. My grandfather used to graze his two cows in Thorndon Park, putting them on leads and walking them down to the park where he'd tether them out on the golf course. Today, Thorndon Park is considered to be one of the most elite golf courses in the country, with a long established history, so how they coped back then with cows roaming along the fairway I'll never know. I can just imagine what the members would say today! (Strangely enough my daughter, Wendy, was lady captain of Thorndon in 2009.)

When I wasn't helping my grandfather on the land, I attended the local village junior school and was there up until the age of eleven. It was only a small school with just three classes and three teachers, but again my youth and naivety meant I was unable to recognise the scale of things or the importance of those teachers in developing me into the person I am today. Miss Bittles was the head teacher, a very strict woman, an old fashioned spinster, and a stereotypical headmistress. She lived in a very nice house in Ingrave and was totally committed to her students and her school. I'm not quite sure whether that was *because* she had no family of her own or *why* she had no family of her own, either way it made her a very good teacher. (When I grew up and eventually got my first farm in Harold Wood, she used to travel on the bus and come and see me, purely because she was so proud of what I had achieved, of what one of her pupils had become… a farmer. My wife, Margaret, always gave her tea and a biscuit and I can still picture her walking up the drive to the house, her face bursting with pride and her eyes wide with awe. There are several things that I regret in my life and one of those is not giving Miss Bittles more time when she came to visit. I almost considered her as a nuisance when she popped by when I had so much work to do, but wisdom has shown me that I should've been grateful that she cared, that she showed such an interest and that she was so genuinely happy about what we had achieved. But then life is about learning from your mistakes, and making sure you don't make them again.)

Chapter 3 – All Change

I had a thoroughly enjoyable childhood; my mother and my grandparents were financially quite poor but as a child I was oblivious to their plight. I felt like the wealthiest boy alive as I ran through Thorndon Park with my friends and played merrily outside in the fresh air. For me, life couldn't have been any kinder, other than having my father back home with us of course. Thankfully the war did eventually come to an end and my father was demobbed back to Essex. Everybody in service with the army was given gratuities at the end of their service; this was made up of the sum of the small proportion of their wage which had been held back each week. The gratuity was intended to be a substantial enough lump sum to enable a soldier to settle back into civilian life, normally allowing them to set up in a small business or to put a deposit on a house. My father chose to use his gratuity to rent a shop in a small village called West Horndon. He decided to turn it into a fish shop and rather rapidly he learned how to become a fishmonger. My mother and sisters moved with him to live over the top of the fish shop, but much to my delight I was allowed to stay with my grandparents. I did of course love my mother and father, and my two sisters, but I also loved the life I was living with my grandparents on the smallholding. I had an extra special bond with them both; as I grew up I discovered that they had lost a son to measles many years before and I think that having me live with them helped them to fill the void that had been left since he'd passed away. So, having me staying on with them in their idyllic little home in the countryside suited both of us extremely well, and I was more than happy with the decision.

My grandparents weren't overly strict, they never hit me, a treatment I know some of my friends suffered, some on quite a regular basis. But my grandparents, luckily, didn't see the need to go to such lengths. They were, as I see it, firm but fair. If I did misbehave I was sent to my room where I had to stay and miss a meal, which I thought was dreadfully unkind at the time. But it was a very good incentive for me. I loved my food and the threat of missing out on my grandmother's home cooking was a big enough deterrent for any misdemeanour I may have been tempted to commit. I tried my absolute hardest not to be naughty, sometimes I failed, but the majority of the time I was good enough.

I tried my hardest at Ingrave Junior School too, but I wasn't particularly bright or clever, which meant I didn't even bother sitting the eleven plus examination. My teachers knew I didn't stand a chance of getting into the grammar school in Brentwood, a very famous school with an excellent reputation which attracted the elite. Funnily enough a lot of the friends I have today attended there, but I was happy to attend the local senior school, which went on to become known as a comprehensive. It was a big school, massive in comparison to the junior school that I had left behind, with a thousand pupils in total, and my first day was a somewhat daunting experience. It was a mixed sex school but the girls were educated at one end of the building and the boys at the other. We were totally segregated for lessons but were allowed to play together during the break times. I'm sure it was quite healthy to allow the sexes to mix for at least some of the school day, although I do remember we had a very long bike shed, complete with lots of bays for those that wanted to become acquainted with the opposite sex a bit further... not that I ever frequented them of course!

Once I had settled in I absolutely loved my time at school, I know the majority disliked it, but for me it was just one of those things we all had to do. I didn't excel academically, I coped with the challenges school brought, but I was never the brightest and in the same vein I was never the slowest in the class either. I was very much 'middle of the road' and happy to be there. I got on extremely well with my peers and also with all of my teachers. I guess my simplistic outlook on life allowed me to get on with others, I tried hard not to offend anybody and I tried my hardest to follow the rules... a recipe for success in your school years. I played cricket avidly throughout my childhood, and as I reached my senior years I was made the captain of the school cricket team as well as being awarded the much acclaimed position of head boy. I actually, rather uniquely held both of these posts for two consecutive years; this wasn't the norm as ordinarily you would only hold the post in your final year, but in what was supposed to be my final year when I could have left at the age of fifteen, the government of the time changed the law such that pupils couldn't leave school until their sixteenth birthday. So, uniquely I led the school and the cricket team for two years running, the only student ever to do so as far as I know. I guess this suggests that I was indeed a bit of a goody goody, but that was the way I wanted to be and in fact the way I still try to be to this day. I like to work hard, I like pleasing other people and I like to do my best, and I think all of those traits, as well as a lot of luck, have helped to get me where I am today.

Although I got on well at school I did stand out as a bit different to the other boys in my class; a lot of them had had quite tough upbringings, and fights in the playground were commonplace, but not for me. I avoided arguments at all costs, partly because I was too scared of getting hurt, and partly because it just wasn't in my nature. I'd never been hurt and I had no desire to hurt anyone else or to get hurt. But the boys that were scrapping were used to that sort of thing, some were very rough, and they were used to having a clip round the ear from their parents, and sometimes more, but I'd had nothing of the sort with my grandparents; it was clear to me that although we were financially poor, we were rich in so many ways. My grandparents always conducted themselves with dignity, being polite and respectful to others, no matter who they were; they were pleasant to everyone and certainly not supportive of fighting or even arguing. I never heard my grandparents argue, ever, and I certainly never heard them swear, as I have never done (I have also never smoked a cigarette or drank alcohol – a fairly unique claim in today's society). My grandfather was a very old fashioned man, he always showed others respect and if he happened to pass someone in the village with any element of standing he would always touch his cap in courtesy and acknowledgment of their position. I often heard him call people 'sir' and it wasn't hard for him to do so; he didn't think it belittled him; it just came naturally, as it does to me to this day. I see it as respectful rather than a sign of being subservient or a lesser person; I guess I got that from my grandfather too… I have a lot to be thankful to both of them for. The way my grandparents brought me up was perfect for me, I couldn't have asked for a happier childhood. It's a pity more children can't be brought up the way I was, because I'm sure the world would be a much better place as a result. Everything that happened to me later in life I believe was shaped by what happened in my early life. My grandparents taught me manners and respect; even when the village policeman came to our house to buy eggs I would cower in fear; frightened of the local 'Bobby', a concept that would possibly have young people today in hysterics. Regretfully though, times have definitely changed, some things of course for the better, but some things, such as the unconditional concept of basic respect for others, should definitely be reinstated in order to make this country and this world a better place.

Chapter 4 – A Padgate Education

My school years flew by and once my sixteenth birthday came around it was time to leave, and the natural next step was to carry on helping my grandfather on his smallholding. One of my jobs was to ride my bicycle out to the pubs in the surrounding villages and collect up all their food waste, taking it back to the smallholding in the cage on the back of my bike, where it was then used to help feed the pigs. It wasn't a pleasant job and as the cage got heavier the journey home got tougher, but I never complained, I just got on with it. I was just like my mother in that respect; she always threw herself into her work, and in fact was more of a business person than my father ever was in many ways. She worked tirelessly from morning till night and thanks to her efforts their fish business thrived. They eventually opened five fish shops across Brentwood, Grays, Romford and Dagenham. I sometimes went back to help out at the shop just to get some wages to tide me over, but I always hated the fish trade and never wanted to go into it. I did my bit out of respect really, showing willing and helping out whenever I could, cycling the seven or eight mile round trip to and from West Horndon just to earn a few pounds.

I think my father appreciated my help, although he never really showed it; he struggled to show any real emotion after he came back from the war. He'd had a pretty rough time there, back then I had no idea just how rough, all I knew was that before the war he was a kind father, who had all the patience in the world, but once he came back my grandparents acknowledged that he was a completely different person, unrecognisable as the man they and my mother had said goodbye to when he went away. Clearly if he'd come back from war in today's time he would without a doubt have been diagnosed with Post Traumatic Stress Disorder, but back then it was just classed as the way he was dealing with a rough time. I now know and appreciate just how much of a rough time being dropped in behind the German lines on D-Day was; he was also part of Operation Varsity and was dropped over the Rhine crossing, then on to Berlin. He was lucky to have survived as two thirds of the men who took part in that operation were killed or wounded. He had certainly had it rough and I can now fully appreciate just how the experiences that he went through would inevitably change a lot of men. My father sadly died at the early age of fifty eight, by which time he had retired from his business due to ill health.

At the age of eighteen it was my turn to do my bit for my country, to sign up for national service. All young men had to do so when they reached eighteen, unless of course they had a very good excuse such as being needed to work on farms; there was no other way out of it. Farming was a very important industry, particularly after the war, and food and crops were obviously essentials, and recognised as such by the government, which was why national service could be avoided for farming men and why farmers were given subsidies to grow crops.

Unfortunately my grandfather's smallholding, with its insignificant acreage wasn't considered essential for supplying the country's crops and food, so I had no option but to sign up. I attended the local selection day where all of the fresh new recruits were gathered to determine which force they would be going into. There were fifty recruits on my intake and about half of them wanted to go into the RAF. The majority ended up in the army, as was the case with most intakes, and of the twenty five RAF hopefuls only three were actually selected, and somehow, rather miraculously, I was one of those three. Luck was shining down oh so heavily on me that day. I was required to attend an interview where I was grilled by several officers; they asked me many questions to try and determine my character, understand my nature and to assess my attitude towards war and our country. They of course wanted to know some of my background and I explained that my father was in the parachute regiment; I believe this was the first element that made them look favourably upon me. It wasn't exactly the RAF but it did involve planes, and a father with an affinity to aircraft and the courage to jump out of them must have stood me in good stead somehow. They then went on to ask whether I was much of a reader and if so what books I read. Just the week before somebody had given me a Winston Churchill book which I had briefly dipped into and read a few paragraphs of. I wasn't entirely sure if I would get away with it but I boldly replied that I was in the process of reading Winston Churchill's memoirs. Much to my horror they then asked me to repeat anything that I had read. I don't know how but after a slight pause I was able to recall and recite back some of the snippets I'd read, which in all honesty were mostly the captions under the photographs. But thanks to that I was accepted into the RAF; luck was truly on my side once again.

After being accepted I quickly commenced my training at Padgate in Lancashire. I had never been away from home before, I'd never even been on holiday; holidays were something for the middle classes, certainly not something that we could afford. I was eighteen and I had spent my entire life with either my parents or grandparents, and leaving them, moving into shared accommodation with fifteen other men, and beginning my journey along the route to becoming a fully trained airman, was a massive shock to the system.

It was January and we were in the middle of a very hard winter. A winter that felt even harder by the time I arrived in bitter Lancashire. I settled, as well as I could, into the billet, and as I always did, I tried my hardest to keep my head down and stay out of trouble. Of the fifteen of us that were housed together, ten of the young boys were from the Gorbals in Glasgow, Scotland. Their accents instantly had me baffled, I couldn't understand a word, especially when all of the Scots were talking together; hearing other Scottish accents seemed to make theirs all the stronger, and I was at a loss trying to understand them. But I didn't need to know every word they said to know that they were tough lads, not the kind of boys that I would choose to mix with in any other circumstances, and not the type that another lad, Bill, who was from Southend, would've chosen to mix with either. He was a really nice young boy, with a public school education, and impeccable manners and elocution to go with it. I got on well with him; he had the same sort of attitude to life and to others as I did. He was gentle, kind, and hard working. But the Scots didn't seem to see that, or maybe they did and they saw it as a weakness; either way he became the target of their vicious bullying. Despite my similarities to Bill I was somehow lucky enough to avoid getting into scrapes, and to avoid being the target of their nasty attacks. I understood that the NCOs and the Corporals needed to be tough in order to do the jobs they had to do, but some of the things I saw from the other trainees were just downright cruel and it didn't sit well with me at all. In all honesty, I didn't realise that such cruel people actually existed. My somewhat sheltered, pleasant, rural upbringing had shielded me from some of the harshness of reality, and seeing some of the things I saw in training was a real wake up call for me.

For the entire first week I cried myself to sleep; I was terrified about getting up in the morning and about what I would have to face that day. I thought I had joined the RAF to work with aeroplanes not to stand by helplessly watching cruel and extreme bullying, and rather naively I didn't realise that I was putting myself forward for the most intense and tireless training regime imaginable. Bill dreaded every day too, but mostly because of his bullies. One night he clearly couldn't face the thought of enduring another day of it, and the following morning he was found hanging from the water tower. He'd killed himself. A young life wasted.

As a result of Bill's suicide we all had to be interrogated by the military police. We were all segregated and accusations and blame were rife. The investigation went on for two whole weeks and we weren't allowed to speak to each other on the subject of Bill's death for the whole investigation period; it was a miserable time. I was petrified that I would be blamed or somehow held accountable as I was Bill's only companion in the billet. I answered their questions as best I could, and much to my relief I wasn't given a tough time over it; I think they could see how disturbed I was by the whole affair. The bullying, the suicide and the subsequent interrogation had again opened my eyes to experiences that I just hadn't ever considered could occur, let alone to me. But the Scottish boys were used to it all, it appeared that they were used to being interrogated too, and they were definitely used to being cheeky, they had an answer for everything; but the police weren't going to stand for their cheek and rightfully they gave them what for at the end of it, although nobody was ever actually blamed for Bill's death. As a result of the massive investigation our normal training period was extended from twelve weeks to fourteen weeks, to compensate for the amount of time that had been spent dealing with the aftermath of Bill's suicide. Those fourteen weeks will be fourteen weeks I'll never forget, every moment of fear, sadness, panic and fatigue individually tattooed on my memory for a lifetime. Looking back on it now however, I realise that all of those things made me grow up very quickly and I learned a lot about real life.

Following training I was sent back down South and posted to North Weald airfield, just outside Ongar; another stroke of luck, it was ideal for me, I was practically back home, and I felt comfortable being back in Essex. After a time of working hard and towing the line I became a leading aircraftsman, and although I wasn't particularly good at figures, I was put in charge of the equipment accounts for 604 City of London squadron, which was a reserve squadron. Following a short period with 604 I was moved to 111 squadron, of which I was very proud. Treble one were one of the first squadrons to receive the Hawker Hunter jet aircraft, whilst all of the other squadrons had either Vampires, the twin fuselage jet aircrafts, or the Meteor, the first jet engine aircraft in the RAF.

Once my early experiences in the force were behind me I thrived in my job and actually had some really fun times. I was even able to continue playing cricket, the sport that I had developed a passion for from a young age. I loved playing cricket and I had an on-going ruse with my teammates; in the 1930s there was a famous cricketer called Jack Hobbs and my opponents and team mates alike all thought I was related to him, and I just didn't have the heart to tell them otherwise, which of course didn't harm my reputation as a cricketer in the squadron. Playing on the wicket that we had cut out on the aerodrome in between the runways was great fun, and my talent for the sport was soon recognised and I was eventually picked to play for eleven group, which covered all of Essex, Suffolk, Norfolk, Cambridgeshire and Kent. Our group would fly off in an Oxford aircraft in order to visit other groups and play competitive cricket against them. The Oxford only really had the capacity to carry twelve people, but we managed to squeeze fourteen or fifteen in at a time and fly off for the day to do battle over the wickets. Yes, life in the RAF was good, and I went on to be promoted to a senior aircraftsman, which meant I could sport a propeller on my arm, and I was able to stay in the luxury that was the sergeant's mess when we were away playing cricket. Life at this time was truly in stark comparison to the horror I had encountered during my time training in Padgate. But I didn't tend to reflect on that time, it was something I chose to forget, I preferred instead to concentrate on the positive, and on the here and now.

Chapter 5 – Deals on Wheels

In my final year in the RAF I was charged with looking after the servicing of parts for the aircraft in the squadron. If an aircraft was to go out of action because of a hydraulic leak or something similar, it was never repaired, instead the part was thrown away and a new part put in, and it was my responsibility to order the appropriate parts as and when they were needed, and consequently my responsibility to keep aircraft serviceable. It was an extremely important role, requiring me to be organised and effective, skills I learned and developed well during my time with the RAF. As time went on treble one squadron became quite a famous squadron, renowned for their three aircraft, all painted black, which they used to perform acrobatic routines. They flew during air shows and became quite a feature of the shows, with spectators in awe of their daredevil feats and synchronisation. As their popularity grew, the decision was made for every aircraft in the squadron to be painted black. I loved watching them practice over the airfield at North Weald, I was mesmerised by the skill of the pilots and the formations they created… but not everyone was happy to be witness to their rehearsals though, the airfield's many neighbours being the main complainants, and in an effort to keep the peace the majority of the practising was done out over the North Sea, where the planes would cause minimal annoyance. Those acrobatic black aircraft from treble one squadron were known as the Black Arrows and were of course the forerunners for the world famous Red Arrows.

Being based so close to home meant I was fortunate enough to be able to travel back several nights a week to stay with my grandparents. I'd take the bus as soon as I had finished work for the day, and make three changes before I got home to Herongate. I loved having the best of both worlds, being part of the RAF and being able to enjoy a more relaxed civilian normality in the evenings. After a good meal and a good night's sleep I would rise again at six the next morning and head out to catch the first bus at seven to ensure I was ready to start work at nine thirty. I certainly lived a full and hectic life as a young man, I worked hard and I made time for the things I enjoyed; cricket and farming. I still loved everything about farming and I still had a simmering desire to be a farmer; I'd wanted to be one since I first helped my grandfather collect eggs on his smallholding, and that desire had never left me. It felt like farming was in my blood and as a result I joined the local Brentwood Young Farmers' Club. Every Monday evening after my bus trip home, I would get on my bicycle and cycle into Brentwood to attend the Young Farmers' meeting. It was a great social event and I wouldn't miss it for the world, even when the rain was lashing down and the wind howling around my ears, I'd make the journey on my bicycle, although luckily I had made some good friends there, and one of them, Peter Ford, would never see me cycle back home again if the weather was too bad. Instead he'd happily put my bike into the back of his Land Rover and drive me back, safe from the rain and the cold. I always appreciated his kindness, made even more pertinent by the fact that he was a farmer's son and I was just a village boy who longed to be a farmer. The chasm between the two classes was significant indeed and yet his kindness bridged that chasm with ease.

I was stationed at North Weald aerodrome for nearly two years, and at the time I had no idea that when I left the RAF I would become great friends with Alan Kerr, another Young Farmer, who farms adjacent to the airfield. If I had known him back then I could have dropped in for tea!

I have always been shown great kindness by all of the Young Farmers, both male and female, and back then I made some great friends there, including a young girl called Margaret Doe, she was two years my junior, and someone that I instantly connected with; not particularly in a romantic sense initially, but as someone that I could converse with, someone whose passion for life excited me. And as we came to know each other, our similarities and indeed our differences brought us closer and closer together.

Unfortunately Margaret didn't however share my passion for cars; I've no idea where my interest in them stems from but I regularly went and scouted around looking for beautiful motorcars. There was a local Ford dealership in Brentwood called Hensman's, owned by a man called Dick May, whom my father used to buy the odd van from. I was often known to browse through the second hand vehicles at Hensman's, looking lovingly at some of the totally unaffordable but exquisite motors that were cleaned and polished until they sparkled. On one of my many visits to look at Dick May's stock I happened to mention to him that one of the pilots in my squadron was looking for a good second hand car. I wasn't really asking for a reason, other than to make polite conversation, and I was totally astonished when Dick's reply was to tell me to take a Ford Pilot (a rather fitting name as it turned out), back to the base to show the pilot and see if he was interested in it. I jumped at the chance… purely because I wanted the opportunity to drive the car. It really was a beauty, and when I got it back to the base the pilot thought so too. I sold it there and then, I think for about two hundred pounds but I can't remember the exact price, and the next day I took the money back to the very trusting Mr May. In return he gave me five pounds, which for me was almost a week's wages; a significant amount of money by anyone's standards in those days.

Unbelievably, about a fortnight later, having seen the Ford Pilot, another officer approached me and enquired about where I had got the car from. I couldn't believe my luck when he asked whether there was another for sale. As soon as I could I rushed back to Mr May's dealership and told him I had another potential purchaser. He offered me a slightly cheaper car this time, and sure enough I drove it away and came back at the end of the week with another sale for Dick. I waited anxiously as he counted the cash and I envisaged another five pound reward; unfortunately he wasn't quite as generous this time around but I still got about four pounds for my efforts; again, a sum not to be sniffed at. My side-line with Dick May soon developed into a regular venture, allowing me to placate my passion for cars, and make some money at the same time; it was the perfect arrangement. He would let me have cars for a fortnight or sometimes even up to three weeks so I could see if I could sell them, and having a car at my disposal meant I no longer had to endure the extended bus journeys home and back, I had the luxury of a vehicle, and often a very nice vehicle at that. Driving through the gatehouse each morning the military police quite understandably assumed I was an officer; they were after all the only ones that could really afford the types of cars that I would arrive in. They'd all salute me as I drove through, and I took great pleasure in not correcting their faux pas. Eventually of course they did get to know me and realise my rank, and the saluting came to an abrupt stop.

I think I sold approximately ten cars in the final year of my national service, I was known as a car dealer, and when I was discharged from the force, with no other career to go to, Mr May very kindly offered me a job as a car salesman. I turned it down, perhaps foolishly for a young man with limited real options, and I'll always remember Dick May's voice resounding in my head as I walked away from the offer, "You'll regret it, boy… you'll regret it!"

Chapter 6 – *Let's Go Fur Farming*

Despite Dick May's warning, I had an instinctive feeling that I wouldn't regret it. I will always say that my time in the RAF was the best thing that could have happened to me; it taught me to get along with all sorts of men and to stand on my own two feet, and it also gave me a lot of time to read as it made the downtime pass much quicker. I liked reading biographies and non-fiction books, I was fascinated by people and their success stories, and one book which I had read towards the end of my service had really got me thinking. It was a book I'd purchased from the local bookshop, entitled *Let's Go Fur Farming*. I can only assume, looking back now, that it was the reference to farming that caught my eye; my connection to farming hadn't left me despite my foray into car sales and my relatively successful military career. I had never previously had a burning desire to learn about fur farming but as soon as I picked up this particular book I was fascinated by the man, the business, the success. Sat in my quarters I buried my head into the pages and finished the book within just a couple of weeks. It detailed how the author, Robert G. Hodgson, had started fur farming in a small way in Canada, catching wild mink and breeding from them. He explained every detail of the process and about how he managed to turn it into a very successful business. It absolutely seduced me, so much so that as I sat and thought about my future as a civilian, all I could think was that, *I could do that too*. Long after I'd finished reading the book, its contents whizzed around my head, infesting my thoughts and exciting me about the potential in the business. It was this seed planted in my head that was one of the reasons I didn't take the car salesman job. And thankfully, once I mentioned that sprouting seed to Margaret and loaned her the book that got me thinking, she felt equally inspired by the idea that fur farming could be the thing for both of us. We were still just good friends at the time but good enough friends for her to take the time to write to the author, Mr Hodgson, and ask him exactly how he started out. She pointed out that on leaving the RAF I was given my gratuity of five hundred pounds, but rather dishearteningly my inspirational author stated quite unequivocally that we needed to start with more stock than my five hundred pounds would buy. I didn't want my dream to end before it had even begun, and luckily my dream had now become Margaret's dream too and she approached her father for a loan of five hundred pounds. Margaret's father was a farmer and contractor. He was without doubt a good businessman, a wonderful father and one of the kindest men I have ever known. He didn't hesitate in putting up the money for the business, and with our joint investment totalling one thousand pounds we bought thirty two mated female mink, and began our farming careers on my grandfather's smallholding. The animals were vicious to say the least; we wore thick leather gloves whenever we handled them, but there were many occasions when we could feel their teeth penetrating the leather and their powerful jaws pressing down into our skin. Presenting the male to each of the females in turn, we watched as they either fought or mated, it could often be quite a chaotic venture, and it surprised me that they only came away with minimal injuries after some of the battles we had to intervene in. It was an exciting time for both of us, we both felt passionately about what we were doing and although we weren't married, or engaged, it felt right that we were doing it together.

We had been working hard at building up the business for a few months and Margaret was looking forward to a well-earned break with the rest of our friends from the Young Farmers who were getting ready for their annual skiing trip. I had never been on the trip, I'd never been able to afford it in previous years, but in this particular year my loyal friend, Peter Ford, had to drop out of the holiday due to his father taking ill. I was over the moon when he offered me his place, especially as it was at the discounted price of seventy pounds all in, which included the flight there, although admittedly that was in a joke of an aeroplane from the small airfield at Stansted as it was then. Nevertheless I jumped at the chance and I'll always be thankful to Peter for offering me his ticket; he like many of the friends I made in my Young Farmers' Club days will always be a friend for life. It was during that holiday that Margaret and I started our courtship properly; it had taken us a while but we were finally a serious couple.

After the holiday it was clear that we were in love, although I'm not the kind of person that would openly admit it. And soon after we were engaged and married. We had a lovely wedding, my in-laws made the day perfect for us, doing everything possible to ensure that we had a day to remember and a great start in life. As a wedding present for Margaret I decided to have a mink stole made up from some of our very own blue mutation mink, which were some of the most expensive. She was delighted with the gift on the day but over time the stole was relegated to the wardrobe and was seldom released. (When we eventually ended our time in fur farming it was clear that I needed a new tractor and I didn't really have the means to buy one, but I managed to negotiate a deal which involved swapping Margaret's stole for a fine tractor… she's never forgiven me, but at the time it seemed like a good idea!)

And so as a married couple we entered into another year of mink farming. In our first year we had successfully bred the mink which produced between seven and ten within a litter, meaning we had built up quite a stock; but we soon realised that there was much more money in selling breeding stock than there ever was in killing them and skinning them; it meant we were diversifying from our original plan, but we were more than happy with that if it made financial sense to do so. At the time there were many mink farms in Scandinavia, North America and Canada, but there were none that I knew of in Britain. I realised immediately that as the only

British supplier we could charge a lot more money for breeding stock compared to a pelt. It had to be done.

I started out with a simple advert in a weekly magazine called *Fur and Feather*. I had responses to the ad almost instantly, with several people wanting to buy stock as well as the cages and equipment to go with it; it seemed like we were definitely on the right track. We also diversified further by buying a few pairs of chinchillas to breed; we had got the idea from one of the mink farms in Canada which was successfully selling chinchillas. We housed them at Margaret's home in her father's barn. It was a great place to sell them from as the first impressions of his lovely old barn always impressed the customers. We were one of the first in the country to start selling chinchillas with their unmistakeable, beautiful soft fur. They originated from the high Andes and were very hardy little animals, and extremely friendly, especially compared to the vicious mink that we were used to. Margaret looked after them for about a year and then we advertised them alongside the mink and found that people were far more likely to buy the chinchillas, and in no time at all we had to source new suppliers to keep up with the demand. There was one particular farm in California which we bought quite a few from. They cost one hundred and fifty pounds a pair and we sold them for two hundred and fifty pounds a pair. We sold so many that we were earning more money with our chinchillas than we ever were with the mink.

Margaret with a chinchilla; one of my favourites!

One of our chinchilla houses

Chapter 7 – Pioneers

In the third year of business we made £9,500, enough to buy our first farm, Ivy Lodge Farm, which unbelievably had a house thrown in for nothing. We bought it for £8,200, which gave us a whole fifty three acres and a house. Adjacent to it was another small farm, Paternoster Farm, which my father-in-law bought for Margaret, I believe for about two or three thousand pounds. The two farms together took our total acreage up to about seventy acres. It was a proper farm, positively swamping the five acres that my grandfather had been nurturing all these years. But the house needed a lot of work, the place was totally derelict before we got our hands on it; there were no proper toilets, just a soil toilet in the garden, and the kitchen was nothing more than just a portable stove. Before we could move in we had to spend a lot of time and money to get it into a habitable state, living for six months in a caravan as we did so. But the inconvenience and the less than ideal living conditions were all part of our next big adventure. We didn't find any of it a hardship, it was exciting, we were newly married, in love and we felt extremely lucky that we had our own farm. And the discomforts and inconvenience we endured for that six month stint were well worth it in the end, particularly as our first child, Sally Ann, was conceived in that caravan!

We worked tirelessly to get the house up to scratch; we installed an Aga which Margaret's mother bought for us and which turned the room that previously just housed a stove, into a proper kitchen. And we really modernised the Queen Anne house, taking out chimneys and fireplaces, which in hindsight we probably should not have done, and putting in new windows and walls. I was twenty four and Margaret was just twenty two and we could already say that we owned and ran our own proper farm. It was astonishing, especially for my grandparents who visited us just once in the early days and who genuinely struggled to comprehend that their grandson, the boy they'd raised, had such a vast farm to his name.

When we moved into Ivy Lodge Farm we moved all of the mink and chinchillas with us, and put up a special wooden shed, a converted chicken shed, to house them. We did very well at our new farm, making about fourteen thousand pounds the following year. But although the chinchilla business was booming, the mink business was starting to die away, partly because of an anti-fur lobby which was causing problems for lots of mink farmers; the radicals were going around letting out mink and forcing farmers out of business. We didn't want to risk it happening to us so we decided to get out as quickly as we could before they got to us. We rapidly ran down our mink stock and simply never replaced them. The chinchillas however weren't considered in the same light for some reason, I sold them as breeding stock, and never actually killed one, but ultimately that was what they were bred for, to get their fur. We had two very good years with the chinchilla, selling them all over the country, advertising in the *Daily Express*, which cost about five hundred pounds at the time. But we always got such a good response from it, it was well worth it.

Part of the mink sheds at my grandfather's smallholding

28

Our success allowed us to expand and diversify even further, a necessity considering the now non-existent mink branch of the business. And so it was that we moved on to farming chickens, erecting two big chicken sheds, housing five hundred chickens in each. With the vast numbers of birds we were able to build up quite a trade at the door for eggs. But I still wanted to try something new; I had always wanted to attempt different types of farming, and with the land we had at our disposal our options were quite open. I decided to move into fruit, something I'd helped my grandfather to grow and knew a fair bit about as a result. I planted up fifteen acres of blackcurrants, clearly working on a much larger scale than I ever had done before, but fortunately I had a solid buyer for my produce in the form of a large jam and soft drinks' company, who produced a squash containing blackcurrants. They bought the first year's crop and it seemed we were on to yet another winner, the luck just kept on flowing… that was until the following year; it was early July and we were just about ready to pick the second year's crop when the agent for our buyer contacted us with a devastating phone call.

"I'm very sorry Mr Hobbs but we can't take your blackcurrants. The government has done a lease swap with Hungary for some machinery, and unfortunately for you, in return they're shipping over tonne blocks of frozen blackcurrants for virtually nothing."

"Right…" I replied hesitantly.

"I'm afraid what I'm saying, sir, is that we won't be needing your crop this year."

I could barely digest what he was telling me. Of course he wouldn't need our crop if the government had wangled it for them to receive the same produce for nothing. But all I could think was that we had wasted a whole two years farming fifteen acres of fruit and we had absolutely nobody to sell it to. I felt panicked. Our market had collapsed without warning and we were well and truly in a muddle. The first big muddle I'd really got into, fortune had favoured me up until this point and I genuinely feared that this was the start of it all going wrong.

But it wasn't to be the end, mostly thanks to a very calm and innovative woman that I was lucky enough to call my wife. Margaret, in her wisdom, decided we should try to sell the fruit to the local residents, and without hesitation she took an old white bed sheet, painted big lettering across the sheet and hung it from the fence at the bottom of the drive; it read: '*Come and pick your own blackcurrants, nine pence a pound!*'

It was inspired, and in her confidence Margaret had even raised the price, charging a lot more than our original buyers were ever going to pay, on top of that we were saving labour costs by getting the customers to do all the hard work of picking the fruit by themselves. This was a brand new concept... we had created the very first 'Pick Your Own'... a phrase that Margaret penned, and that worked as beautifully then as it does now on farms across the country. I advertised our pick your own scheme in the *Barking and Dagenham Post* and the *Romford Times*, which reached a lot of Asian families who lived in the area, and they flocked to come and pick fruit at our farm. And indeed they were experts at it, with practically every punnet picked being only the best fruit from the crop. The majority of the other local residents had to be shown how to pick, with most of them still struggling to find the best fruit and taking their time to fill a punnet. But, all in all the venture was a resounding success, our near massive failure had been turned around overnight into a pioneering and exciting new business opportunity and business boomed.

We then expanded into strawberries and raspberries, once again using the 'Come and Pick Your Own' approach, and advertising all over East London. At weekends we had thousands of people coming to pick fruit, and we were so busy that we had to employ four or five car park attendants to control the thousands of cars that descended on us, as you can see in the following photographs.

Car parking for 'Pick Your Own'—over thirty acres of cars

Blackcurrant 'Pick Your Own'

Strawberry 'Pick Your Own'.

On a good weekend we would have over two thousand people coming; mainly from the East End of London.

One of our frequent customers was a local businessman, Sir George Chaplin. He owned a big estate agency business in Romford, and he used to arrive in his chauffeur driven Armstrong Siddeley motorcar to buy strawberries. As his car approached along the drive I always made sure I was the one to greet him. He never stepped out of the car though; instead his chauffeur would exit and be the one to announce that he was looking to purchase a tray of strawberries. Of course, I always made sure that I dug out the best fruit for him, and doing so seemed to ensure that he came back, time and time again; he was definitely one of our loyal customers. Unbeknown to me he did in fact own a farm himself and it was almost adjacent to mine in Upminster. His tenant there however had proved to be a poor farmer, with a lot of the land being left to go derelict. One day as I prepared myself to hand over another tray of fruit I was taken aback to see Sir George Chaplin get out of the car himself. I wasn't quite sure why, but when he announced that he'd like a word with me, I most definitely felt nervous, and I wondered whether the last batch of fruit hadn't been up to scratch. But it turned out it was just the opposite. He had been visiting my farm for two years now and he was impressed with the work we had done on it. So much so that he was now here with a proposition for me. He was there to ask if I would be interested in taking on his farm, Chapman's Farm. I was like a small child who'd been promised an amazing birthday present, I practically bounced from foot to foot with a stream of, yes Sir, no Sir, yes Sir, flowing from my mouth.

And so it was that Sir George Chaplin let me have the tenancy of Chapman's Farm, it was two hundred and thirty acres and was only a mile away from Ivy Lodge Farm where we lived. It was in a very, very poor state and my landlord, Sir George, unbelievably gave me the first two years rent free, and even after that I only paid a very fair rent of about eight to ten pounds an acre for the next two or three years, I had landed on my feet... again!

Chapter 8 – The Equestrian Era Begins

When we first took on Chapman's Farm it was in a pretty dire state in terms of the land and the buildings, most of which were far from fit for purpose, other than an old cow shed which the previous tenant had converted into four stables. He'd been letting out the stables to local girls with ponies, and I decided to carry on letting them and allowing them to keep their ponies there, charging them just two pounds fifty a week. I put up a new barn within which I could house my corn and run my farming operations from and converted the existing barn, which was very rundown, into an indoor riding school, which the four girls could use in the winter. I hadn't bargained on the stables being any sort of real business enterprise for us, but the girls that rode there soon told their friends about us and subsequently we had enquiry after enquiry from people looking for stables and wanting to keep their ponies at Chapman's Farm. I responded to the demand and built another forty four stables, it was a big step up but I knew we could fill them. Developing our stables so that we became the largest livery stables in the area proved to be a very profitable leap to take, with the horses more than paying the rent. Plus it was a DIY business, the type that we had become very keen on; we supplied a tack room for everybody's tack, and bins for everybody's food but after that the business pretty much ran itself. We were also able to sell them hay and straw at premium prices.

Although surrounded by horses I had never had the urge to ride myself; that was until one of my tenants, a horse dealer, was struggling to pay his rent arrears for the five stables he rented from me; his arrears now stood at over one hundred pounds.

"Look Eric, I've got a nice horse here; I'll give you the horse instead!" he pleaded with me one afternoon.

"I don't want a horse," I replied.

"But he's a beauty, go on try it," he urged.

I could see he was desperate and I took pity on the man, and the horse, which was a pretty plain looking horse, but there was something about him, and I agreed to take it. The dealer loaned me a saddle and I had a ride, playing about with him in the indoor school. He was a totally honest horse and would do anything I asked him to do, he would go anywhere and jump anything and I soon found that together we could actually have quite a bit of fun.

From this point on I grew to love riding and now I had a steed I was able to join my friends out hunting; my hunting companions in those early days were two brothers named John and David Tucker, they owned a television and electrical business in Hornchurch, they went out hunting regularly and once they heard I had a horse they invited me to join them. I thoroughly enjoyed everything about hunting, the energy, chasing about on other people's land, the rush; and after that first weekend I became hooked. My children loved riding too, Sally was the first to have a pony and she got on very well with it; she joined the East Essex Pony Club and made several friends there. Malcolm wasn't quite as eager to ride as Sally was though, and I practically had to force him onto a horse. I bought him a pony, even though he didn't really want one, but it meant that rather than being left at home twiddling his thumbs he had the opportunity to come out riding with me, and when he did, he loved it. I went on to buy all of the children ponies, and they all spent many happy days riding out in the fields, tending to their horses at the stables, and having fun with the Pony Club, making some great friends along the way. As a family we had a lot of fun riding, every weekend Margaret and I would travel across East Anglia to attend a horse show with Sally and Wendy, or to go show jumping or hunting; none of us particularly wanted to catch foxes though, we just wanted to enjoy riding across the land,

and we had great fun doing it. As time went on we all became heavily involved in the Pony Club, which allowed us to make a lot of new friends, some of whom we are still friends with to this day. But as soon as the children got old enough to make up their own minds about what they wanted to do, the novelty of riding wore off and they all decided that the opposite sex was far more interesting than ponies.

I have always thought that horses are great levellers of men as they have no respect for wealth or any titles a person may have; without a doubt horses bring everyone back down to earth and I'm glad that I and my family had the opportunity to experience the joy of riding.

Our lives were good ones, we were working hard and enjoying family life simultaneously, something that not many people can achieve. Everything was going well for us once again, but as I had learned from the near miss with our blackcurrant buyer, I knew my luck could change at any time, and it did, with our chickens being struck with fowl pest, not just once, but twice. It was a devastating blow and we had no choice but to inform the Ministry of Agriculture who sent people out to kill all of our birds. Our second infestation occurred whilst Margaret was pregnant, and our local doctor had to pass by the men tasked with killing the birds when he came to the house to deliver our son, Malcolm.

The curse of two doses of fowl pest was enough to put Margaret and myself off of chickens for good and we decided instead to try our hand with breeding rabbits. I went to see a top executive at Sainsbury's who was acting as a buyer for them at the time. The manager from the store in Brentwood who arranged the meeting with the buyer, had said that he could easily sell bred rabbit meat because the only rabbit meat he could currently source was wild rabbit, which the customers were not very keen on because it had shot in it. My farm reared rabbits would be the perfect solution and they agreed to stock my rabbit meat in Romford, Brentwood and Ilford. We once again advertised in our old faithful, *Fur and Feather* magazine for New Zealand white rabbits, which were big and excellent converters of food into meat. And Margaret and I subsequently drove around in our Austin pickup truck to buy up the rabbits that were offered to us by the sellers who had responded to our ad. We loaded them into the mink cages in the back of our van, brought them home and housed them in the deep litter sheds where the chickens once were. We had everything in place and the rabbits, well they did what rabbits do, and our stock soon multiplied. Once again it all seemed to be taking shape with our new line of farming, but once again tragedy struck, in the form of myxomatosis. It killed the rabbit trade overnight and I was left with hundreds upon hundreds of rabbits which nobody would buy. And so, having dug a hole for the chickens I now had to do the same for the rabbits. Although once buried I struggled to keep them down there as the urban foxes would come night after night sniffing them out through the soil, and digging them up to eat.

We had certainly had a run of bad luck but I was never one to dwell on that, perhaps it was because the good luck outweighed the bad luck. Whatever it was, throughout all of the drama, even with pits of dead livestock buried outside the house, I still felt like the luckiest man alive.

Chapter 9 – A New Home

Next to my farm was Upminster Common, where there was about one hundred acres or more, upon which couples used to drive their cars onto and do their courting. A relatively harmless pastime for the young couples who really had nowhere else to go in those days, but in the winter months it wasn't always straight forward for them as the common became very boggy and muddy, and cars very often got stuck. As my farmhouse was next to the common I was the first port of call for young men (although they were not all young) in their hour of need, who very often had a pretty girl waiting for them in their car that was stuck on the common. They would wake me up in the middle of the night and I would let them know it would cost five pounds to pull their car out of the mud with my tractor. Considering a farm hand's wage at the time was about ten pounds a week, it was a sum worth getting up for in the middle of the night. It proved to be a very profitable venture, and I used to look forward to it being wet because it was a dead cert that somebody, if not everybody on the common would get stuck. In a reasonable week I could earn ten to fifteen pounds per day from my car recovery service, but when the weather was really bad I could easily make one hundred pounds a week. And the extra money came in particularly handy after I had a rather nasty accident involving some bales of hay falling on me which dislocated my shoulder, it was excruciatingly painful and I had my arm in a sling for quite some time, which meant it was difficult for me to work. But one job that I could still manage was to drive out in my tractor and rescue the stuck courters night after night at one and two o'clock in the morning. It was the perfect way to survive through my injury and a very interesting little side-line. I could tell several interesting stories about some of the awkward situations couples got themselves into, but it is not that kind of book!

Very often the people I rescued weren't able to produce five pounds from their wallets, after all, it was a rather hefty sum to be carrying around in cash, and today, as I write this book it amazes me how five pounds seems so little money. But even if they didn't have the hard cash on them I still had a way of getting the money out of the stranded young lovers. If they weren't able to produce five pounds on the night I used to take their watch as security, and I never had any complaints for doing so. They would then come back over the next few days with their five pounds and I would subsequently return their watch. Remarkably when we eventually sold Ivy Lodge Farm I had a clear out and found a drawer full of watches, all of them obviously a lot cheaper than the five pounds that they were held in security for.

One summer evening we invited my friend Barry Webb and his wife round for supper, Barry was a local builder who stabled his horse with me. We enjoyed a lovely meal and as the night went on the conversation veered onto discussing the possibility of any residential planning on our land. There were two fields butting up to existing houses and Barry thought there would be a good chance of getting planning permission because of it. We finished our coffees and Barry's wife and Margaret went into the lounge to relax and catch up, whilst Barry and I stayed firmly seated around the dining table. After a few minutes our conversation waned and Barry's face became more serious, as though he had something significant to announce.

We got up from the dining table and made our way into the kitchen to talk some more.

"I just wondered," he paused, "Would you be interested in selling your farm?"

"Yes," I said without hesitation, "Providing the price is right."

"Oh right, well, how much do you want for it?" he asked, seemingly shocked at my quick decision.

I hadn't really thought about it before and so had no real figures to work from but I started high, "One hundred thousand pounds," I said, not dreaming it was anywhere near worth that amount.

"I can't give you that," he scowled. As I knew he would.

Instead, the sale price was eventually agreed at ninety thousand pounds, not exactly far off my original asking price, and in 1965 that was an awful lot of money.

I could not believe I had sold the farm, just like that, there in my kitchen, but it was a done deal and I was overwhelmed with Barry's offer.

Ivy Lodge; in 1956 we bought fifty three acres plus this house for £8,200

As far as I'm aware Barry never actually moved into the farmhouse as he already lived in a lovely house in Elm Park. And as far as I'm aware he never got his planning permission either, but I do know that he sold the Queen Anne farmhouse for a very good profit several years later, so he more than got his money back. Barry went on to become a hugely successful businessman and is probably the wealthiest man I know, largely, I imagine, as a result of his hard working ethics and an eye for a good deal.

With the knowledge that we had about one hundred thousand pounds (once I'd added Barry's offer to the sum we'd already saved) to play with to purchase our next farm, Margaret and I went out looking for a new home, and the world was pretty much our oyster. We travelled to Ireland to look at two farms over there; land there was very cheap in those days, the 1960s; I could have bought a thousand acres, not necessarily all farmable as it was very poorly drained, but still it was a lot of land. But Margaret wasn't really that keen on such a big move, so we focused our attention back in England. We looked at a nice farm in Shropshire, another in Somerset, another in Sutton Hoe near Woodbridge, but nothing was really ticking all the boxes for both of us.

At the same time my father-in-law's company was trying to sell Earls Colne airfield, which they had bought a few years earlier. My father-in-law used to manage airfields as a civilian contractor during the war, so he knew a lot about them and post-war they were all being sold very cheaply. He had a fair bit of interest in Earls Colne but eventually he made a deal with a local buyer, but right at the last moment they pulled out, we were never sure whether it was the masses of concrete that they couldn't face or the poor state of the airfield generally, there were thorn bushes over it, and the drainage was very bad where they had levelled it all off; it certainly wasn't going to be an easy project to take on for the new owners. But with four hundred and fifty acres for sale and his buyer dropping out, my father-in-law suggested that Margaret and I take it on. It was a wonderful opportunity and we both jumped at it and purchased it from his company.

An aerial photograph of the airfield during the war

Marauder of the 323 bomb group which was based at Earls Colne for over two years

Marauder flying over Earls Colne airfield

Brave men returning to Earls Colne after a mission

Bob Hope and Frances Langford performing at Earls Colne

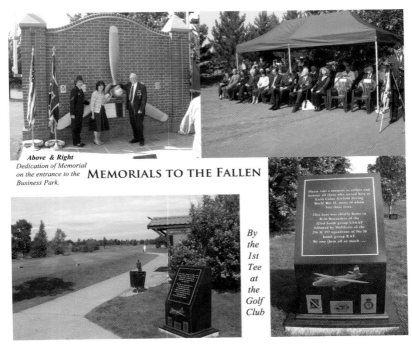

Above & Right
Dedication of Memorial
on the entrance to the
Business Park.

MEMORIALS TO THE FALLEN

By
the
1st
Tee
at
the
Golf
Club

A memorial service held at Earls Colne

45

New airfield memorial to war dead

by NINA MORGAN
nina.morgan@nqe.com

A FORMER prisoner-of-war has returned to the Earls Colne airfield where he served with the American air force and unveiled a memorial to his fellow airmen.

Bob Mims, 86, was a pilot in the US Air Force (USAF) and was stationed at Earls Colne during the Second World War.

Mr Mims was shot down during a wartime mission over France and survived a crash landing only to be captured by German forces.

He was taken as a prisoner-of-war to a stalag near the Caspian Sea and was held captive for 15 months.

Mr Mims was freed at the end of the war and made an emotional return to the airfield, now Earls Colne Business Park, on Wednesday, where he was one of the guests of honour at the memorial unveiling ceremony.

He was honoured with a 21-gun salute by members of the USAF, based at RAF Mildenhall, at a ceremony attended by almost 70 people.

The war veteran then helped Captain Michael Murphy, of the USAF 100th Refuelling Wing, to unveil a new memorial at the entrance to the business park, dedicated to the airmen who fought, and in many cases, died for freedom in the Second World War.

Braintree MP Brooks Newmark, who also attended the unveiling, said: "It was a very moving ceremony.

"It was good to see the US Air Force around, celebrating the service that their predecessors did."

The event was organised by Sally Blackwell, whose father Eric Hobbs bought the airfield originally to farm in 1965, and Master Sergeant Bert Guillot.

She said: "The day went really well. Unfortunately, the planes didn't fly over for the planned flypast, though."

After the unveiling ceremony guests and dignitaries enjoyed a reception at the Essex Golf and Country Club.

● Unveiling – Captain Michael Murphy, of the USAF 100th Refuelling Wing, during the ceremony surrounding the new memorial.
(57632-7)

● Guard of honour – colour-bearers from US Air Force parade during the ceremony.
Pictures: LOUISE MORRIS (57632-8)

Newspaper coverage of the war memorial service at Earls Colne

The memorial to all the airmen who gave their lives so we could be free

There was no house at the airfield, but our good builder friend, Barry, the new owner of Ivy Lodge, offered to build us a brand new house for ten thousand pounds. The house that he created was a nice five bedroom home which gave us everything we wanted and more, and where I still live to this day. And no matter how much money I have, I will never move from that house, in fact the thought of living in a regular, ordinary house, absolutely horrifies me; I love living there, I love the house, the garden, everything about it, and it was all created from a flat, arable field as you can see in some of the photographs.

Deciding where to build our house (September 1966)

*Honeywood Farm (March 1967), which cost just
ten thousand pounds to build in 1965*

The same house with an established garden and offices (2012)

A view of the garden with the Monet Bridge at the far end
and the offices on the right

The garden in full bloom

An aerial view of Honeywood Farmhouse

The Monet Bridge and gardens at Honeywood Farmhouse

The airfield itself was in a bad state of repair, the landscape blighted with heaps of concrete made from areas of ripped up runway. I sold the majority of the concrete on to various companies, and a large proportion of it was used to make the Marks Tey bypass. One company in particular bought a great deal of my concrete at three hundred pounds an acre; again, when I compare those prices to the sum of one hundred and twenty thousand pounds which I paid for just one acre of concrete to be laid in 2011, it really is shocking. I sold about fifty acres of concrete in total, in hindsight it was a silly thing to do but it was money coming in when I needed it most.

That money allowed us to build stables, one of our priorities once the family was housed. We built a block of six stables to house Margaret's horse and the other two horses which I had now accumulated, and once our horses were moved over from Upminster we continued to pursue our passion for riding. I rode about four days a week, either hunting or just exercising my horse on the grounds of Marks Hall estate. I came to an arrangement with the estate that I would give them the right to use my roads on the condition that they let me ride my horse on their land, which was about five hundred acres of woodland; the arrangement worked very well for both of us, and they have proved very good neighbours. So, with the house built, the stables constructed and the horses in their new homes, we then concentrated on working out what to do with the four hundred and fifty acres that we had taken on. Initially we farmed it, but because of the poor condition of the land, after every harvest I had to take a cultivator to pick up any stones that were left from the runways and roads that had been previously taken up. I always got the children on board to help, even though they hated the job, in fact to this day Sally still mentions the fact that she has scars on her hands from where shards of stone cut her during those tedious stone picking days. But eventually our cumulative hard work paid off and the land became a much easier place to farm. And with the quality of the land improving year after year we decided to start another 'Pick Your Own' scheme at Earls

Colne, selling gooseberries, raspberries and blackcurrants. Sally was in charge of the selling and she was very good at it, but as competition increased and supermarkets started pricing us out of the market, selling seasonal fruit all year round and at prices far cheaper than we could offer, it was inevitable that that branch of our business naturally faded away.

Despite this we made a good living from farming, which allowed my children to go to private schools and allowed me to hunt in Leicestershire two days a week. I went on to hunt for about ten years with the Cottesmore, twice a week during the winter; I also stabled horses there at Melton Mowbray, and on Saturdays I used to hunt with the East Essex. Writing this now I realise I must come across as a bit of a playboy, but it was only during the winter when we weren't particularly busy on the farm. We even set up our own little shoot on our farm, joining up with our neighbour Bill Waters and his son, Robin. Bill used to look after the game and for about ten days during the season we'd set up a friendly farm shoot, and indeed we made lots of shooting friends during that time who are still my friends today.

Shooting at home in the early 1980s; (from left to right) Roger Norris, Peter Ford, Robert Cole, John Powell, David Smith, Robin Waters, Dick Blackwell, Bill Waters, John Blackwell, Me, Richard Carter

We really did live a marvellous life; things couldn't have been more perfect. Our love of horses and riding prospered further and once again the Pony Club became a steadfast part of our lives, with me going on to become the District Commissioner of the Pony Club for about five years in the early eighties.

Chapter 10 – Industrial Revolution

The airfield became a massive project for me, and whilst I was assessing new ways to develop the land I was approached by a young man called Clive Ripper who came to ask if he could base his business, C R Timber, at Earls Colne. I agreed and he moved into one of the existing Nissen huts.

I continued to develop the farm putting up a large building of twenty thousand square feet in total, with the intention that I would use it as a potato store, which I did for a year. But then I was approached by Peter Bingham-Wallis who was looking to set up in the agricultural machinery business, and was looking for premises to conduct his business from. He was very experienced in the industry having previously been the owner of a company called Eastern Tractors, the Massey Ferguson main tractor dealers, which had just been sold to Tom Cowie. I had no idea how he found out about my barn, but I knew he was keen about business, and determined to make his venture a success, and I was keen to help him do just that. After a few initial discussions we approached the relevant authorities to see if we could get planning permission to convert an agricultural building into an industrial building, and thankfully for him and me, we could. After a few months his business was born, as International Harvester, which was actually a large American company which manufactured agricultural machinery, but they had no dealership in the South of England so he became the face of International Harvester in the South, and he was very successful with it too, and the rent soon covered the cost of the building. And with Clive Ripper's business and International Harvester established, I had my first taste of industrial buildings, and I was hooked.

The only original building on the site, apart from a few small Nissen huts, was a large hangar, which I had actually paid for separately when I bought the airfield. I used to do everything in there, I had grain storage in one end, and we let out three quarters of the hangar, about twenty thousand square feet, to The United Sack Company, which was the biggest sack company in the country, making its money from hiring sacks out to farmers at harvest time. They paid me eight hundred pounds per year, which considering the original cost of the hangar, was a lot of money, in fact the hangar soon paid for itself.

Soon after the International Harvester company was up and running, another company, Milbank Floors, approached me looking for somewhere to site their business. They made concrete floors and were based at Great Waltham just outside Chelmsford, but they had been receiving lots of complaints about dust and contamination where they were. They had decided to ask Braintree Council if there were any sites where they could carry out their manufacturing without causing what was seen as a nuisance because of their twenty four hour working and the dust produced; the reports suggested that their business had made life pretty unpleasant for their neighbours. Soon after their initial enquiry one of the council planning officers came along and had a look at our site, as we were the only people living there, and as we owned the site, if I agreed to find a home for them I didn't really have any grounds to complain if they became a nuisance. I did agree, and the Milbank family came and set up business in former horse paddocks, creating a large manufacturing plant and offices. They have been here ever since and have been very successful, and still are one of the largest concrete beam and floor manufacturers in East Anglia and possibly the country. At their peak they were employing about three hundred people all at Earls Colne, and I am still yet to find their business a nuisance! And that was how I grew from one converted potato store to building more and more factories. To date (2013) we have about five hundred thousand square feet of industrial and business space, and the total rates bill is over one and a half million pounds. I must say that I feel very fortunate to be in the Braintree district, as not only have I had great support from the local people but I also have a very supportive District Council and Parish Council.

I employed my own people to build the units and factories, and I got subcontractors in to do the work that my own builders couldn't do. Mark Graham was a young lad who had been in the Pony Club when my children were there, and when he left school his father asked if I could give him a temporary job, just until he could find a proper one. I agreed, not knowing that he would still be here nearly thirty five years later, I assume still waiting for a proper job to come along; but Mark has been a great employee, he can turn his hand to anything and he now manages the business park. In the late eighties I took on another young man, Robert Ely, who came by on his moped, aged seventeen, looking for work, he too was hoping for a proper job, but in the meantime was willing to help me out as a temporary measure until a good job came along; he's still here too! He is also very involved in the construction of new buildings and is now our construction manager.

The working team in 2013: (from left to right) Mark, Gavin, Mickey, Bob and Malcolm

The units kept on going up and they kept on getting filled with new businesses that were keen to snap up the buildings as soon as they were finished. I worked very closely with an agent called Andrew Crayston who was working for Abbots estate agents at the time, in the early eighties. He helped me tremendously with the design and layout of the business park and he, Malcolm and I spent many hours talking to the planning officers at Braintree District Council, and without their support and the support of Earls Colne Parish Council, the development of the airfield to the point it is today, would never have materialised. Andrew is still working closely with us, albeit that he has moved several times and is now seeing out his days with Fenn Wright in Colchester, where until recently he was senior partner. I know that he is very proud of his involvement with both Malcolm and me, and we both owe a great deal to him and his words of wisdom.

We have, at the time of going to press (2013), about thirty different companies on the estate including ABL Doors & Windows Ltd, Brochure Holders, Bulldog Aviation, N.C. Cammack, A1 info, Electro Assembly Services Ltd, Trane (Ingersoll Rand), Fleetshield, Hullmatic, David Watson Transport Limited, Woodland Group, Multitek, Result Clothing Ltd, Soprema UK Limited and Stourbridge Water Direct. We also have The Ford Motor Company, which brings cars off the production line and converts them into police cars, converting thirty to fifty cars in a week. They have parking spaces for over five hundred cars, with virtually all of them being full on a permanent basis. In 2012 we were also joined by Wilkin & Sons, the Tiptree jam manufacturers, probably one of the best known privately owned companies, in not just Essex but in England (you can find their jam on the breakfast tables of most good quality hotels across the country and the world). One of the smaller successful businesses on the estate is the Essex Dentistry Clinic, as well as my granddaughter's business, Evergreen Clinics, which offers physiotherapy, osteopathy, sports massage and a Pilates studio. Our most high profile tenant however is Essex Air Ambulance whose administrative offices are here, along with Hertfordshire Air

Ambulance; their helicopter is also based here on the airfield, and all of the proceeds of this book will go to them to help keep the helicopter flying; I know it saves lives. The airfield is operated by Mick Manders who started flying here over thirty years ago with just one aeroplane. However, he has now developed the airfield into a fully licensed CAA airfield and a thriving business, which goes under the name of Anglian Flight Centres. The centre trains pilots for commercial aircraft as well as those just looking to fly for pleasure.

The airfield as it was in 1996

Earls Colne airfield (2012) operated by Anglia Flight Centres which offers flying lessons and pilot training. There are custom facilities for those who wish to fly into Europe.

Trevor Avery, whose company Multitek was another original tenant has also been operating a very successful business for the last twenty five years. We also have Baxters on the estate, who are the country's leading soup makers, and our biggest tenant Vislink (Gigawave) which manufactures and supplies television antennae. Vislink produces the antennae that transmit the signal from the camera to the satellite, enabling the picture to reach the television set. Vislink are a multi-million pound business, supplying equipment for the last four Olympics and supplying countries all over the world, which also means they have always got clients coming from abroad, who conveniently stay at our hotel on the golf course when they come to visit. In our peak in 2006 to 2007, we were asked by Braintree District Council to do a survey to calculate how many people actually worked on the business park; we found the park was employing around fourteen hundred people, which took us all by surprise as we had no idea that so many people actually worked on the estate, although that figure did of course include part time employees.

We developed the business park into a very successful business, which allowed me the freedom not to have to work so hard, and gave us the opportunity to have a decent holiday once a year, having not had one for seventeen years. It also meant we could run a decent car; I have had Range Rovers since 1969 when they were first produced, and my original Range Rover cost £1,900. I have just taken delivery of my eleventh Range Rover (2013) but I won't reveal to you just how much it has cost because Margaret would be very cross indeed!

All we ever wanted though was to provide a decent living for both Margaret and I, and our family, and so far that's what we've achieved. The estate is something we are all very proud of, and it is managed by Malcolm and Sally who are doing an excellent job.

A selection of photographs which tell the story beautifully...

Margaret's parents, Florence and Herbert Doe

Margaret's family (1946)

Brentwood County Secondary School Cricket Team

*Mrs Hobbs (Mother), Sheila Hobbs (sister), Mr Hobbs (Father), Me,
Marie Hobbs (sister)*

*A Young Farmers' dance; Margaret with her friends
Gillian Speakman and Pat Flemming*

Promoting mink and chinchilla at the Essex show (1958)

Picking apples at Margaret's father's orchard at Diggens Farm (1956);
this was our first business venture together and
we made five hundred pounds

I've always liked a clean car

My pride and joy… the first car that Ford sold for one thousand pounds, I told you I had a weakness for cars! (1957—before we were married)

Mr and Mrs Eric Hobbs on our wedding day (1958)

*My parents (Walter and Joan Hobbs), the happy couple, and Margaret's
parents (Herbert and Florence Doe)*

Margaret holding Sally (1959)

Sally and Malcolm on Tommy, in front of Ivy Lodge Farmhouse (1964)

The farm at Upminster, putting straw in between the strawberry rows

A picnic in Honeywood Avenue, Marks Hall

The children ready to ride (1972). (From left to right) Wendy, Sally, Malcolm… I'm not sure about Julian! (Front)

Half term 1972—the family with Nicola Blackwell hiding in the background on the chestnut pony

Wendy on Mountie (Gosling Cup)

Malcolm on Noddy and Eric on Trampus

One of my best horses, Golden Lad

Going hunting at a local meet (another lovely horse)

Sally on Sea Spider; she won many competitions on this super pony

*The Four Colnes Show, held at Earls Colne Business Park
for several years*

1970's

*Malcolm on a new
Ransomes combine*

Potato picking by hand

1980's

*I didn't really need two combines
but it looked impressive!*

Farm building being converted for International Harvester

Jim Cammack's storage building being built; since moving here Jim has built up a major logistics company

Oriental Hotel, Bangkok: our silver wedding anniversary

Margaret and I in Andorra with Ann Carter (1985)

Myself and Richard Carter (1985)—he still has more hair than me!

73

My mother's civil dinner with the family—she was Mayoress of Brentwood District Council; Julian was none too pleased!

Julian (ski instructor) taking the family skiing (1988)

74

The newly built office in my garden (1997)

More serious moments with Malcolm and Sally (it was all staged really)

Summer party in the garden for the Conservative Party

In the garden—my retreat

Margaret and I on holiday—I wish I had some of Margaret's hair!

Outside Buckingham Palace with my mother, Margaret and Sally. My mother had just received her MBE for serving as a Conservative District Councillor for over thirty years

The stables

The Essex clubhouse with the hotel on the right hand side

The view from the hotel circa 1999

An aerial view of the business park and both golf courses plus the driving range in the foreground

*Business park and golf course with Earls Colne village
at the top of the picture*

Milbank Floors' offices and factory yard

80

*Baxters' new factory; I used the money I received from the sale of the
Upminster farm to build this factory for Baxters*

The entrance to the estate

Vislink (Gigawave) offices; Waterside House

The whole family at Amy and Craig's wedding,
in Sally and John's garden (2011)

*On my mower with my granddaughter Amy's house in the background;
she moved into this house in 2011, after her marriage*

Standing in the Ford car park, before they moved in

Fairways office building, resident swan and golfers

Fred, another nice horse!

Prospect House on a frosty morning. This is one of the buildings that we own on the Skyline 120 development in Braintree

Golf course 13th hole; I do like my bridges

Julian's house being built at Henley-in-Arden, Warwickshire

Some of the industrial buildings on the business park

*The Fairways office building which overlooks the
nine hole garden golf course*

Pond and trees on Halifax Way

Wilkin & Sons Ltd, famous for their jam, moved here in 2012

Baxters, famous for their soup, have been on the estate for many years

One of the Ford buildings

David Watson Transport grew from just one lorry in 1984, when he worked for Milbank delivering their concrete floors. Today he has a modern fleet of over one hundred vehicles based at several depots across the country, with about twenty five vehicles based here on the business park

Our security vehicle and the gatehouse

*Family and friends on a skiing holiday. (Back row, from left to right)
Danny Watts, Andrew Crayston, Myself, Sally, Holly, Liz Inskip, Carole
Watts, Chris Milner-Moore. (Front row, from left to right) Sam,
Malcolm, Janet, John*

Myself with Malcolm and his family

Janet and Malcolm plus Rafi, 'the guard dog'

Julian and Ali (2011)

Julian, Ali and Bethany at the Olympics 2012

Julian with Bethany (2012)

Some of my grandchildren; Rebecca, Emily, Victoria, Ben and Felicity in the pool at home

Malcolm and his family with Sally's sweet peas in the background;
Ben, Janet, Malcolm, Rebecca, Felicity

Four pretty granddaughters

On our golden wedding anniversary, Margaret and I plus chocolate cake
(one of my weaknesses)

Two photo's of the Business park area taken 15 years apart ...... Graphically illustrating the total transformation of the area, with improved landscaping, amenity areas, and employment creation.

Before and after 1988 - 2003

96

The whole family (not including Amy) celebrating fifty years in business

Surviving fifty years in business 1957 - 2007

Summer lunch with friends (2012), all from our days in the Young Farmers; we have known them all for over fifty years

The head gardener mowing the lawn

John, Sally, Wendy and Jeremy on holiday together (2011)

Victoria Steel and Oliver Blackwell's wedding – Victoria's parents put on a lovely wedding

Sam Blackwell and Holly White's wedding – The Whites put on a super wedding at Marks Hall

Wendy and her family

Festive lights as you come onto the estate at Christmas time

Chapter 11 – Up in Smoke

Devastatingly though, on April 22nd 1986 the good life that we were living was put dramatically in the balance when fire broke out in our large warehouse. I had taken a young boy on a few weeks previously, who was the step-son of a woman who used to work for us picking up potatoes. She had been a hard working lady and she mentioned that her step-son was drifting a bit, and wondered if he could have a job with us. I offered him a temporary job, and on this particular day I had given him the task of tidying up the potato store which was adjoining the large warehouse where Gerbers were storing tinned salmon and jars of jam for Sainsbury's. He was a nice lad and he did as he was asked, pushing all the leaves and debris into a heap in the corner of the store. He then set about his next task which involved grinding some metal, but disastrously the sparks from the grinder flew out and landed on the heap of debris he had gathered, and it instantly took light. The fire spread rapidly, partly because it was a particularly blustery day but mostly because one of my sheds was lined with polyurethane for insulation.

I was at the Upminster farm when I received the devastating call to say that the farm shed was alight, and with it a lot of my farm machinery which had been stored in there, including three of my best tractors, our new combine harvester and all the potato planting equipment. Luckily however the seed potatoes which were ready for planting were being stored elsewhere. But by the time I got home it wasn't just the farm shed that was ablaze. There had been a forklift truck in the same building, which had a gas cylinder lying horizontally on the back of it. The flames caught the truck and inevitably the gas cylinder exploded, firing out like a canon straight through the potato shed and into the shed next door, igniting the Gerbers' store of imported jams and the like. There were millions of cardboard boxes in that warehouse and the whole place went up in a very short while.

As you can imagine, by the time I got to the scene there was very little we could do other than stand back and watch in horror as the twenty-five fire engines tried their best to tackle the unforgiving flames. It was absolute chaos, not only from the flames, the thick smoke and the fire engines, but also from my phone which was ringing non-stop. But one call that I will always remember from that night was one that came from Peter Philpot, who I actually didn't know very well at all back then. Peter had heard about my fire and that I had lost all of my potato planting equipment and he was ringing to let me know that first thing in the morning he would be sending over two men and his potato planting machinery, so that I could still plant my potatoes. That was thirty years ago but I still remember his kindness to this day, and since then I know he has continued to help many of his friends in their hours of need, and we all say that under his distinctive loud voice he has a heart of gold. "Peter, I hope we meet in heaven."

Thankfully nobody was hurt during the fire but the resulting fallout was that Gerbers' insurers sued me for five and a half million pounds. I was only insured for one million pounds, which in short meant I was facing bankruptcy. My whole world, my family's lifestyle, everything we had worked so hard for was about to come crashing down around us, because of one fateful spark.

EAST ANGLIAN

Wednesday, April 23, 1986   **DAILY TIMES**   No. 35,533   Price 22p

Food store devastated in £4m blaze at farm

MORE THAN 160 firemen yesterday fought a farm fire at Earls Colne in which £4 million damage was caused.

By Simon Penfold

Crews from as far away as Sudbury, Ingatestone and Harlow were called to the blaze at Honeywood Farm on the Coggeshall road.

The men, some wearing breath apparatus, took four hours to contain the blaze.

In that time the flames devastated a large farm workshop, containing about a dozen vehicles, and a neighbouring warehouse ‑ruining about £2 million of tinned foodstuffs inside.

Farm owner Mr Eric Hobbs said he had lost seven tractors, four forklift trucks, a new £68,000 combine harvester, potato machinery and about 100 tons of potatoes.

He had lost all his main farming machinery which

would affect operations "very badly" for the rest of the year.

"As long as nobody's hurt, that's the main thing," said Mr Hobbs.

He owned all the warehouses on the site and leased them out. The one hit by the fire was leased by food distributors Gerber International Ltd.

Although an ambulance and a doctor were at the ready, they were not needed.

The fire started in the workshop and spread to straw covering the potatoes, said Mr Hobbs.

The neighbouring ware-

house was affected and a huge cloud of smoke rose above the farm and drifted over nearby Earls Colne airfield.

Firemen travelling from Great Leighs, about ten miles away, could see the smoke.

As the fire ripped through other buildings, there was a series of explosions as propane gas cylinders ignited.

Firemen summoned reinforcements. Ten, then 20 and finally 25 fire-fighting vehicles arrived at the farm, with more than 160 men tackling the blaze.

The heat was so great that paint melted on the tin sides of the warehouses.

The fire in the workshop was soon under control but

Continued on Page 11

Burnt-out farm machinery in the workshop where the blaze started.

The fire made front page news

My only godsend was that I was insured with the NFU Mutual insurance company, and as part of that insurance I was covered for any legal costs. My own family lawyer, Tony Frost, recommended that I go to the top London Lawyers, Herbert Smith, who were and still are famous litigation lawyers. I left it in their capable hands to try and find a way out of the lawsuit. But whilst I had confidence in their legal prowess, the threat of bankruptcy loomed over my every thought; it was a very harrowing time. But rather than dwell on the prospect I decided to use my time productively and I spurred myself on to build more and more buildings, as much as I could so that if I did lose the case I could sell some of the buildings and have enough money to still stay in my house and the farm, even if I lost the commercial side of things. Luckily Margaret Thatcher was in power and she gave small businesses the confidence to grow and expand, so my new buildings were actually very easy to let.

And so life and business carried on whilst the lengthy legal machinations started their slow progress. One morning I happened to read in a magazine that a university had carried out a survey and found that there was a need for seven to eight hundred more golf courses in the United Kingdom. Golf was an elitist sport in those days and the courses in existence were nearly all members' courses, with most of them having very long waiting lists for members. In fact my own son, Malcolm, was on the waiting list at Gosfield golf club. Having read the report something told me that Earls Colne could be just what the golfers ordered, even though I knew that an airfield wasn't really the ideal place to put a golf course, it was flat, had no trees or even anything remotely interesting on the landscape, as you can see in the following photograph, in fact it was far from ideal, but the idea still lingered on regardless.

Farming Earls Colne; just one field of one hundred acres. The whole airfield was flat like this field. 1987 – the year before we started building the golf course, not the most interesting of landscapes

Coincidentally, the man that had carried out all of my drainage work on the airfield was a friend of mine called Ted Watson, who owned a company called Anglia Land Drainage, which had just started out building golf courses. And with nothing to lose I asked Ted to come and have a look to see if he thought a golf course at Earls Colne was a viable option. In all honesty he wasn't really too sure but I think he wanted the work so we went ahead and looked into it anyway. Ted suggested that I got a designer to come and design a course, and when I started looking into it I found that there were plenty about, but the only problem was that they all wanted fifty thousand pounds or more just to design the project, that was before any plans had even appeared. It seemed extortionate to me, but another stroke of luck intervened just at the right time which meant I wouldn't have to part with anywhere near fifty thousand pounds.

I had been at infant school in Herongate with a chap called Reg Plumbridge, his father had been a golf professional at Thorndon Park, and Reg, a professional golfer himself had just started out designing golf courses. I happened to hear about Reg's new venture and decided to ask him how much he wanted to have a look at Earls Colne, and as I anticipated, he offered to do it an awful lot cheaper than anyone else in the business. After initial discussions we decided not to rush into anything and instead chose to do a little market research by putting a golf driving range up first to see how it went down with local golfers. Sally ran it and the uptake was phenomenal, we made fifty thousand pounds profit in the first year, but more than that, we had gained the confidence to go and spend millions on a full, eighteen hole golf course, plus a nine hole, par thirty four course.

And so, in 1988 I went to my bank manager at HSBC, Jeff Higgins, in Colchester, and presented him with my plans. He considered them politely before trying to let me down gently, "Look, we're doing one or two golf courses at the moment and we're not looking to do anymore…"

"You know I've got a good track record with you financially and I've got about a million pounds to put towards it myself," I interrupted.

Jeff thought for a moment, "How much do you want?"

"Well, to start with, three million. Although I'm not sure if that's going to be enough," I added.

He considered my proposal for some time before finally agreeing that we could have three and a half million. But of course he couldn't agree to such a deal without getting his superiors involved, and the following week they came down from London and joined myself, Margaret and Jeff around my dining room table. There we brokered a deal, agreeing there and then that they would lend me three and a half million pounds on a twenty year loan at a fixed rate of nine per cent, and I had to put the business park up as collateral. Unfortunately interest rates dropped right down to three per cent during the loan term. But a deal was a deal and it was good enough for me.

In 1991, as I expected, I needed to take out another loan, and thankfully, once again the bank agreed. With the money in hand I then had to make an agreement with Ted and his new company which he had set up specifically to build sports grounds. And Ted didn't disappoint, he did a great job, and as the golf course materialised we all felt very proud of what we had created. Ted was so pleased with the result he went on to build his own course, Benton Hall, which is now run under the same company as The Essex.

When I first arrived at Earls Colne in 1965 there were no trees anywhere on the whole estate, not one, everything had been flattened, but luckily I had the foresight to start planting and I spent a lot of time and money putting spinneys in. And so by the time the golf course was being developed I already had an abundance of ten and fifteen foot trees in the spinneys. I even bought a machine from America which moved large trees and I spent a further three years meticulously moving them all around the course.

*Alan Doe (Margaret's cousin) who supplied all
of the golf course machinery*

Julian with the tree planting machine I bought from the USA

My established trees gave me a good fifteen year head start on others who were building golf courses at the time, and now, when players wander out onto the course it is hard for them to believe that it actually exists in the middle of an airfield. I have planted many thousands of trees of different species, and they provide shelterbelts on what once was a treeless prairie. The trees are beautiful, and well established, as if they have always been there, and I am extremely proud of them, we have even won several awards for our tree planting, as well as conservation awards, and an award from Braintree District Council for the design of the new control tower for the flying club. The work we have done to make the estate appear so naturally beautiful is very important to me, and I am so vested in the trees that I make it my responsibility to look after them on a day to day basis, even though the golf course itself is now leased out to another company, the trees are my domain and cannot be touched without our permission.

We started building the course in 1989, initially building the course and the clubhouse, and we opened it on May 1st 1991. Andrew Crayston, who had been so instrumental in helping to develop the business park also contributed a great deal when it came to designing the clubhouse, in fact the whole building was conceived in one afternoon as he and I sat in his office making sketches; we submitted the plans to the planning office immediately afterwards and the final building strayed very little from our original idea.

We ran the golf club ourselves for five years; Sally was in charge of everything inside the clubhouse, with Margaret helping her where she could, Malcolm looked after the green keeping and maintenance, and I generally dipped my nose in everywhere.

The club Summer Ball (1994)—Sally organised an annual ball for many years

In fact I committed a great deal of time and effort into the golf club, partly to take my mind off of the impending legal court case, which, after a very long, drawn out process, spanning over five years, had finally come to court in the Royal Courts of Justice in London, also in 1991. The case lasted a fortnight in duration, with us all being required to take the stand in the witness box to say what we had to say, including Malcolm; and when it came to the judge's summing up he stated that Malcolm had put his case very well. That five years, and in particular that two week period was the most worrying time in my life, but, we won the case and we could all start to sleep soundly again; luck had continued to fall down on our side. NFU footed the entire sum of the lawyers' costs which were over one million pounds altogether and I couldn't have done it without them or the sharp Herbert Smith legal team I had. They were so clever and their intelligence and extensive knowledge made me feel terribly inadequate; their thought processes, the way they delivered their arguments, were just phenomenal; if left to me to fight my own battle the outcome would have been the polar opposite. Their argument was not based on us not being negligent, because we clearly were, as I was ultimately responsible for the work my staff carried out, but our legal team focused instead on the role that the polyurethane spray had to play in the fire, and in particular that it was sold to me as being non-flammable, when in actual fact, it went up like a bomb, and once it got going there was nothing that could put it out. There had been a previous case in Paris, France, where they had used polyurethane to stop the noise getting out of a nightclub, spraying the entire building with it to make it look like an underground cave, with stalactites etcetera; but just like my barn, when fire struck, the place went up as if dowsed in petrol and unfortunately in that case, thirty people were killed. The judge at my case said that it should never be sold in its current form and definitely not sold as a non-flammable product (the company that manufactured it went into liquidation soon after). And my extraordinary luck had seen me through yet again.

After the court case, a celebratory lunch at NFU Mutual HQ with my family and three of the NFU's top executives

Chapter 12 – New Management

With the case behind me we could carry on with our lives, a great pressure had been lifted and hopes of a calmer future lay on the horizon. Everything started falling back into place and things were going really well once more, that was until 1995 when I suffered my first small heart attack. It was at this point that my doctor told me that I needed to change my lifestyle or else I would be dead within six months, mainly because I was a workaholic and a terrible worrier, even with the court case closed it seemed I still found things to worry about. I took a step back and looked at my life and my work, and Margaret and I realised that I would have a lot less stress if I didn't have to worry about the running of the golf course. It was then that we decided, for the sake of my health that we needed to lease the golf course out. A large company called American Golf said they were interested in taking on the lease and we arranged a meeting with one of their directors in Carolina, USA. Unfortunately at the time Carolina was in the midst of one of their most horrendous thunderstorms and everywhere was flooded, including our hotel; and the man we were supposed to meet was unable to get through the storms and the floods to come and meet us. But whilst we were there hauled up in our room, Malcolm telephoned and informed me that we had a famous celebrity who was interested in leasing the golf course and that he sounded like he was going to be a good bet. It sounded perfect, and with American Golf looking less and less like an option as the rain continued to pound down, Margaret and I came home and agreed to meet up with this celebrity on our return. The celebrity that Malcolm was talking about was Eddie Shah, the founder of the UK newspaper, *Today*, and the man who took on the print unions and won (I should have realised he was a tough man to deal with).

We held several meetings with Eddie to discuss doing a deal with him, and while we were negotiating he came across as quite a reasonable chap, although he certainly had a hard edge about him, I assumed that was what made him a successful businessman. We finally agreed a price and a twenty five year lease and once the contracts were drawn up I took them to the golf club office so that we could both sign on the dotted line. It was on that day, as soon as the ink had dried on the contract, that I became privy to the real Eddie Shah. He had been using my office for nearly a month whilst we had been doing the deal, phoning the United States, using my secretary etcetera, at no cost to him, but as soon as we had shaken hands and the lease was officially signed over to him, his attitude changed. He became a very difficult tenant. I know he was never happy being a tenant, he always wanted to buy the freehold but as we were under no pressure to sell and the family certainly didn't want to sell, we had to live with him. He renamed the golf club from The Earls Colne Golf and Country Club to The Essex, which we did not approve of at the time but the name is now so established that it remains in place today.

After five years Shah received an offer from a company called Club Haus, an English company with a German name. Club Haus were the operators of about twelve clubs nationwide and they were willing to give Shah several million pounds for the lease, and he picked up his money and went. But despite the difficult times we experienced we did learn a lot from him, and in actual fact it probably did us a lot of good because it hardened us up to the realities of the real world.

Unfortunately, not long afterwards the new tenants, Club Haus, went bankrupt, and were taken over subsequently by Legal and General Investments, triple A tenants. They went on to run the course for a couple of years, before selling it to an Irish investment company called The Club Company, who are the owners of most of the eleven or twelve golf clubs that they operate. We got on very well with all of the post-Shah tenants, and now we refer to his time with us as simply an unfortunate episode in our lives. The Club Company are still the current tenants and have proved to be very good ones, paying the rent without issue and running things in the best possible way. I help them out when I can, and we all get on very well together. There have been several different managers along the way but all in all we have been very happy with them. Although strangely I am yet to meet any of the owners, a group of Irish businessmen, in fact, I am yet to even know their names, having only ever dealt with their chief executive or their finance director, who again we get on extremely well with.

The course itself has developed quite dramatically from its original state of being when it was just a golf club and a driving range. It had originally started as a pay and play golf club, but after a couple of years we found a lot of people wanted to become members, particularly the ladies, and so we obliged, offering a membership option for those that wanted it. We now have a thriving membership; the men's and ladies' sections compete in all of the Essex competitions, and all sections have proved very friendly, with long lasting friendships being formed within them. There are also societies that come from far and wide on an annual basis, with many coming back year after year. As well as the golf course there is also a very large gymnasium, a tennis club, with six indoor courts as well as three outdoor courts; the whole complex just grew and grew as we kept adding more and more facilities, and there are currently over three thousand members all together (2013). There is also a crèche which a lot of people on the estate use, and a forty two bedroom hotel which is also very successful, with last year (2012) producing seventy four per cent occupancy for the year, which is a more than respectable statistic. We also hold weddings here, which have proved very popular, and we now have two or three weddings every week during the summer months. The whole site evolved into a country club rather than just a golf course, and we were employing nearly a hundred people including part timers; but luckily the responsibility of running it was no longer ours.

The loan that we took out to pay for the two golf courses and all the other facilities, six million pounds in all, was finally paid off in June 2011 and we made every single payment on time throughout the whole twenty year period; as a thank you for sticking to my part of the deal, HSBC bank took myself and my family out to Le Talbooth for lunch, not really what you would expect from such a large financial institution in this day and age, but then again we did earn them an awful lot of money.

The golf course is now twenty two years old and we are all very proud of it; there is no money owing on it, and I have been very fortunate that I have not had to sell anything along the way to get by. However, I am in a very lucky position that means I am able to give things away, for instance in 2009 I gave the village about three acres of land for allotments. Seventy one allotment plots went overnight and there is now a waiting list for others who want to try their hand at growing their own produce. I like to try to help the village when I can, and a donation of land allowing people the opportunity to get out in the fresh air and farm like I did as a boy, seemed like a great way to do it. The small amount of arable acreage that I have left is farmed by my good friend Peter Fairs who is a very successful local farmer; I say local, he does in fact farm half the county!

As well as doing our bit for the local community with regard to the allotments, we were also given another opportunity to help when we were approached by the School of Advanced Drivers in 2007. They asked whether they could have the use of our estate roads for young underage drivers, namely sixteen year olds who weren't yet allowed to drive on public roads. We have about four miles of our own roads that we maintain to a standard as good as the public roads, if not better, and when the driving school put their proposal to us we thought it was a great idea and said we would give it a trial run to see if they could get enough interest in it from parents. The response was phenomenal and now every third Sunday of the month is fully subscribed with young people wanting to get their first taste of driving. We have places for two hundred and fifty youngsters, with fifty instructors each time, culminating in over 2,500 lessons each year, an unbelievable amount, and we have young people coming from as far away as the Midlands, Kent, Surrey and London; we understand it is the largest such scheme in the country. We make no charge for the use of our road system as we feel that if the scheme saves just one life then that is payment enough.

The Young Drivers Scheme established at Earls Colne—the instructor's car park

In addition to our driving scheme we also allow local schools to hold cycling events on our roads on several Sundays during the summer, to help raise money for school funds.

We were also approached by Coggeshall Cricket Club, asking if we could help out by providing a cricket ground for their second, third and colts teams. As I was very involved in cricket in my early years I decided to build a proper cricket ground with pavilion for them.

Opening of Cricket Field & Pavilion June 2007.

Coggeshall Colts; the cricket ground has been a great success

Me umpiring a game of cricket; we built the cricket ground and pavilion for local players who were finding it difficult to get a game at weekends. It is used most weekends during the season

Chapter 13 – Today

Whilst I was developing Earls Colne I was still the sitting tenant at Chapman's Farm; I had originally taken the farm on as a tenant in 1961 and held the tenancy for over thirty years, and in all that time I had never had any visits from the Chaplins, they were the perfect landlords, and I presume that they were content with the way I was farming it; I treated it as my own, I took pride in it, and it proved to be a very lucrative farm, with us growing over a hundred acres of strawberries and raspberries there. We subsequently renamed it 'The Strawberry Farm', as it is still called to this day. We also started a farm shop in the eighties, again being pioneers of the concept, but I leased the shop out as it was hard work trying to run it when we were not actually living on site.

But in 2003 Sir George Chaplin's son, Sir Malcolm Chaplin, decided it was time to sell up. As a sitting tenant he gave me first refusal on the purchase; I accepted the offer and bought the farm for about four hundred and fifty thousand pounds.

Initially I appointed a manager, Kenneth Coe, who lived in the farmhouse and managed the farm shop and all of the people who stabled their horses there, which was an art in itself. He had an easy way with people, could talk to anybody and managed to extract stable fees much better than I ever could. He looked after everything very well including selling the sixty or seventy acres of potatoes that I was growing at Earls Colne. We had a custom designed trailer and large tractor which Ken would use to come and collect twenty tonnes of potatoes at a time to take back to the farm shop to sell, and very often he'd have to come back twice in one week because he'd sold out. He averaged thirty or forty tonnes of potatoes every week during the winter, which was an astounding amount. Ken managed The Strawberry Farm for many years, but unfortunately he was diagnosed with motor neurone disease, and from the onset of the disease to the moment he died it was just six months.

At that time I had my hands totally full with Earls Colne and I needed someone to take over from Ken, and so I decided to give my daughter Wendy's husband, Jeremy French, a tenancy on The Strawberry Farm. He continued to farm the land and run the stables very successfully; Jeremy is a very good farmer. But after a time I realised that farmland had gone up significantly in value and eight years later I decided to sell because I thought I could make better use of the money that was tied up in the land. I advertised it with Sir Malcolm Chaplin's firm, Hilbery Chaplin, who were selling agents, and along with Strutt & Parker it was eventually sold. I had received lots of offers for it in the time that it was on the market, but the best offer I had was from Trinity House College, Cambridge; it wasn't necessarily the best offer financially but it worked for me. They wanted it as an investment, and I sold it to them for three hundred thousand pounds less than I could have done if I had sold it in small lots to different parties, but the reason I did so was because Trinity House agreed that my son-in-law, Jeremy, could continue to farm the farm on a commercial tenancy, providing that he paid the normal commercial going rate to them, as he still does today. It suited us all, and despite the discounted asking price, I still sold it for about one million pounds more than I paid for it, and of course I put that money straight back into erecting more industrial buildings.

It was a good deal, something I normally cannot resist, but there are some deals that no amount of money will make me accept... Just before the Lehman brothers collapsed and the credit crisis loomed, I had an enquiry from a London firm of commercial agents regarding the Earls Colne estate. They had received an enquiry from a major overseas institution that wanted them to try and find good commercial investments, and they had been asked to look at the whole Earls Colne estate, both the business park and the leisure facilities. They had got a lot of details from Companies House, and as a limited company they would have had access to my company accounts going back many years, so it was totally transparent that the rents had been going up and up over time, in fact, the rent roll at the time he came to have a look at the site was over three million pounds annually (2007).

More out of curiosity than any real intention to sell I asked them to give me a valuation of what the whole estate would be worth, and they gave me a figure of between thirty five and forty million; their response stunned me. I lost several nights' sleep worrying about what to do; we all had such a good lifestyle as it was, and if we didn't have the estate we would all have to go our separate ways, and although all of my children would have been multi-millionaires, quite truthfully, I knew and still know that money alone doesn't bring you happiness. It's nice to have enough but not to have too much. I also think it does people good to work for their money, rather than being handed it on a plate; you appreciate it far more if you have had to work for it. It is seen time and time again with lottery winners, some are sensible but some squander it, not that I am suggesting that my children necessarily would have squandered it, in fact I am absolutely sure they wouldn't have. The other issue which saw me keeping quiet about the valuation was that I didn't want to give up the fabulous working relationships we all had. I've always felt so lucky that I've been able to work alongside two of my children, Malcolm and Sally, seeing them every day is a joy, and Sally, Margaret and I even take time out every weekday morning to go for a coffee, somewhere different every day. We are very fortunate in that we have very good farm shops, garden centres and the Tiptree tearooms quite close to us, so we have a good choice for our coffee and cakes; I love it because it is quality time together; it's simple but I treasure the experience and I wouldn't want it to change. If the estate had been sold, the chance of our family staying quite so close together would be a very slim one. I also asked Colin Tiffin, who was my accountant (as his father was before him) to work out how much capital gains tax I would be liable for if we sold up. He came back to me after a couple of days of research and stated that it would be in the region of seven and a half million pounds, which very quickly helped me make up my mind… no sale. (E Hobbs Farms Ltd was no longer considered to be a farming company by the Inland Revenue, for tax purposes it was treated as an investment company.)

Admittedly if I wanted to sell the estate in today's economic climate (2013) it would be a very different story as commercial property has weakened considerably since the collapse of the banking system (although I'm sure it will come back given time). But even so, I still have no regrets whatsoever about my decision to hold onto it and the lifestyle that it gives us. And I appreciate every day just how fortunate I have been in getting to this point… a far cry from the cramped bungalow I shared with my extended family as a young boy.

My dear grandmother who had opened up her home and her life to me as a young child, died at the age of eighty six, after spending her last years being cared for in a home following her diagnosis of Alzheimer's; when she passed away she left me with lovely memories but she left very little in the way of material things. My grandfather lived to be ninety two, and when he died he left four hundred pounds which came about from a shilling a week insurance policy. (I can still remember being a young boy and seeing people coming round the village collecting the shillings without fail each month.) Four hundred pounds wasn't really much to show from a life of hard work but that was how my grandparents were, they were happy with their lives and they never borrowed any money (I think I have made up for them on this point). They were very content with their lifestyle and although my lifestyle is blessed with more material goods than they both had, I take pride in the fact that my values, morals and sense of family are just as theirs were. They were the ones that gave me those important elements of my character and I owe them an awful lot; one of my regrets in life is that I never thanked them enough for the happy years I spent with them, from four years old to twenty years old… I owe them so much; I owe them who I am today.

I have very few regrets in life, in all honesty, but another that I have is that I gave up riding my horse when I did. After my heart attack in 1995 my health deteriorated somewhat, and in 2009 I had to have a triple heart bypass operation, aged seventy four. As I was being discharged Margaret and Sally asked the surgeon who carried out the operation whether I should give up riding, and his reply was simply, "Well he should be old enough to make his own mind up but my instinct is for him to say he's had enough riding."

With his words ringing in my ears I came home and my horse was sold. I do regret that now, I was a bit hasty, particularly as I feel so fit and well, and the riding was a great form of exercise for me, plus I loved it. Of course at seventy eight I am far too old to start it again now and so I suppose I just have to be grateful for the fact that I was lucky to ride for as long as I did, which was over fifty years.

After my bypass operation I retired from the day to day running of the whole estate and Malcolm took over, which he continues to do much better than I could especially with all the new technology which makes today's business world a very different one to the one that I'm familiar with. But Malcolm is very comfortable with it all, and has expanded the business in the last few years, acquiring property in Braintree at 'Skyline 120', and a fifty per cent share in property in Norfolk and Suffolk with his friend Joe Read, and I am sure he is going to be very successful with it; he works very hard which is always a good indicator for success.

The office for the business park is adjacent to my house which is very convenient for all the family. Lisa West has been our secretary for the last ten years and she keeps both me and all of our books in order, and is an important part of running the business and our affairs; she is a great asset.

I think we are pretty unique as a family, especially having Malcolm, Sally and two of our granddaughters living on the estate with us. And, importantly to me, everybody still works, and I hope they will all continue to do so. We all live a very happy life, and I sincerely hope that continues to be the case even after Margaret and I have gone.

Chapter 14 – Margaret's Memoirs

Of course, my life would not have taken the direction it has if I hadn't met Margaret along the way, and I feel it's a necessity that she gets to put her side of things in this book, which is all about the life which I have shared with her for over fifty years…

I, Margaret Doe, was born on the 27th February 1937 in the bungalow at Ernest Doe's, Ulting. At just a year old my family moved to Pickerells Farm in Fyfield, where my father, Herbert Doe, opened a new branch of Ernest Doe (my grandfather) & Sons. In 1939, not long after the move, my younger brother Robert was born, completing our family along with my two older sisters, Evelyn and Sheila. We all had a wonderful childhood, running around on the land and doing our bit to *help* on the farm, although looking back and with the hindsight of parenthood behind me I realise that our help was probably more of a hindrance. My mother, Florence Doe (nee Poole), was kept very busy by all of us and life was pretty good for all of us too. Which was why, in October 1944, when we were hit by a Doodlebug, it was hard for my mother to uproot the entire family to move to another farm, Boyton Hall in Roxwell (which is now owned by a friend of ours, Peter Philpott). I was seven at the time and although we were only there for eight months I made myself at home quite quickly and had great fun exploring the large house and riding my bike up and down the long drives.

But life for me changed again within a few years, and at the age of twelve I went away to St Monica's School, in Clacton-on-Sea, to stay as a boarder. I loved my school days, I had lots of friends and played in all the school sports' teams; sport was my thing, I loved competing, the comradeship, everything about it, and I threw myself into every possible sporting opportunity. At seventeen I left school and went to a London secretarial college which, as it turned out proved a great asset to Eric and I in our business. And after leaving the college I got a job as secretary to the clerk of the governors at Essex Agriculture College. This suited me just fine as all of the students were Young Farmers and I pretty much knew everyone there. At this stage I too joined Ongar Young Farmers and I became heavily involved in the Young Farmers' social events, and it was at this time that I met Eric.

After two years Eric and I married on November 3rd 1958. My parents gave us a lovely wedding in a Marquee at Pickerells Farm and the day was absolutely perfect in every respect, and our honeymoon that followed was an insight into the way our life was going to be from now on; we travelled to the West Country, collecting debts for chinchillas and as a result we came home with more money than we started with… Eric Hobbs, the only man you'll ever meet who made a profit on his honeymoon!

Once back at Ivy Lodge we settled into married life and it wasn't long before I became pregnant. During the next year, before Sally was born, *Pathé Pictorial News* made a short film about us and our fur farming. It seemed very strange seeing ourselves on the cinema's big screens but then what we were doing was quite unique especially in the UK, so it was understandable that there was such an interest in us. After the media attention died down, Sally was born in September 1959 and her brother Malcolm arrived in October 1960. His arrival coincided with an outbreak of fowl pest in our chicken shed; it was a difficult time for us, but we worked through it and came out of the other side busier than ever.

In 1964 Wendy arrived and I truly had my hands full with three children, office work, farming and selling eggs at the door. Which is why I was so grateful for the help of Mrs Hewitt, she lived in our cottage and was a massive help to me in all aspects of my life. In

1966 we moved to Earls Colne; it was a big move for us, and one that seemed like a real adventure, from picking the spot for our new home, which we named 'Honeywood Farm', to spending many hours picking up stones from the muddy garden to be, which is now a beautiful serene spot all thanks to Eric's hard work; it was all well worth it.

In 1970 Julian arrived, completing our family; by this time Sally was now eleven years old and cherished the moments she got to help out with the new baby.

As all the children grew up they all developed a love of ponies and we bought each of them their own pony, and they each took an active role in the local Pony Club. They had lovely times with their ponies and their Pony Club friends, but because of our farming activities we could never get away for a proper holiday, so in 1976 Eric and I decided to put in a glass covered swimming pool so that the children could really enjoy the summer, and it was a great hit. Our neighbours, Cecil and Mollie Blackwell farmed alongside us. We soon became friends, Mollie and I walking our prams together, then sharing school journeys etcetera. We also played tennis together for many years and now play golf together, a long lasting friendship.

The children were all very sociable and it was no surprise that they also became great friends with our next door neighbours. Sally played with Nicola Blackwell and they used to go for long pony rides together in Marks Hall woods. Malcolm played with Howard, mostly around the farm. And they had a younger son, Martin, the same age as Julian and the two of them used to go pond fishing and camping together. Fortunately Wendy had Penny as a close friend; Penny's family, David and Blitz Smith, farmed at Stisted and the two of them played and went riding together. And as well as having fun on their horses and roaming around the farm they all helped out too, once they were old enough to do so. They drove the tractor carting corn and potatoes, as well as helping in the fruit fields behind the tills, and throughout the winter we graded potatoes from the store in our shed, although none of the children liked doing this particular job.

Unfortunately, as a family we've all been a bit accident prone, Eric broke and dislocated his shoulder in 1964 and Malcolm had his toes badly cut in an accident in 1965. Wendy broke her arm when she was seven, when her pony, Moonbeam, stumbled in a rabbit hole. Then at the age of ten she had a bad fall off her pony at Woodbridge Horse Show; sadly she ruptured her spleen which had to be removed, and she was in hospital for a week. As her mother I felt terribly sorry for her and very guilty for letting it happen, but Wendy was determined that her fall wouldn't change a thing and she still continued to ride and went on to win lots of events. But that wasn't the end of our accident report card, sometime later Sally tripped and cut her face quite badly, requiring her to have stitches, and then Julian fell off his bike and broke his arm. Not to be out done Eric fell off his horse and broke his arm too and I fell off my horse and broke my wrist. Sensibly I decided horses were dangerous and from then on I just kept to my dogs.

Eric also went on to have a particularly nasty accident whilst adjusting his irrigation machine and ended up in hospital with a broken back. Looking back it sounds horrendous but it all just seemed to happen and we all just seemed to deal with it.

Throughout this whole time we remained good friends with all the Young Farmers and still are to this day. Peter and Elizabeth Ford, Roger and Jane Norris, Robert and Ann Cole, and Ken and Madeleine Howard were particularly close to us, and from 1980 we all used to go away for a long weekend together at the end of February. We used to take it in turns to organise it and Jane Norris was very good at organising our weekend outings to museums etc.

Eric and Ken used to hire horses and go hunting on the Saturdays, and whilst staying at The Imperial Hotel at Torquay the staff made a real fuss of them when they came down to breakfast in their pink coats, although they were not so keen to do so at teatime when the men came back mud splattered! Sadly, for health and death reasons we stopped our weekends away. However, in 1983 we bought an apartment in Andorra, where we used to go and stay for skiing holidays which became an annual event.

The gang on holiday (2000) Peter and Elizabeth Ford, Ken and Madeleine Howard, Roger and Jane Norris, Robert and Ann Cole, plus Margaret, with me taking the photograph

In Barbados with Peter and Elizabeth Ford

In 1991 when we opened the golf club it was my job to start up a ladies golf section. We did have a few members who had lessons at the driving range and they helped me to get things up and running. I got in touch with the Essex Ladies Golf Union, who very kindly came out to see me and with their help a committee was formed which paved the way for what is now a large section with an average of thirty five to forty members playing in our weekly competitions and strong teams playing in the county competitions, some very successfully. However, it is the friendships which I most enjoy and feel proud to have been a part of, as well of course as the success of the ladies section.

As the children entered adulthood their lives started to take very definite directions, Sally qualified as a secretary and after college went to work in the office at the Spastics Society home at Wakes Colne. It wasn't long before she fell in love with another one of our neighbouring farmer's sons, John Blackwell. They were very young and got married before she was twenty one. They lived at Fordham for a while where Sam was born. Not long afterwards two farm cottages near Honeywood Farm were put up for auction and Eric, with Roger Norris on our behalf, bid and bought the pair. These cottages became, and still are, a lovely home and garden for Sally and John, and after a few years Oliver and Amy arrived to complete the family.

When Malcolm finished school he went to Hadlow College for Horticulture and Agriculture. He worked for six months at Peter Ford's to gain experience, although he didn't particularly enjoy this as they had a dairy herd and he had to be up early to help with milking, which didn't sit well with him. However, he is a hard worker and he and Eric farmed the airfield together very successfully.

All of the children went to Young Farmers, and had a very good social life there, and it was there that Malcolm met his wife Janet Ferguson. Her mother had lived near me in Ongar and we had both played hockey together and been members of Ongar ladies hockey club. Malcolm and Janet live in a converted barn on the airfield and they have Ben, Felicity and Rebecca.

Wendy went to London to study beauty, and then opened a salon in Coggeshall; she met Jeremy French, also at the Young Farmers. He lived and farmed at Billericay which is where they now live and they have two girls, Emily and Victoria.

Julian, several years younger also went to Horticulture College but he decided to go his own way and now lives in Warwickshire where he owns several holiday lets. He married Alison Riches and they have a daughter Bethany.

Eric and I are very fortunate as we see our children, grandchildren and now our great grandchildren regularly, we all get on famously together and our swimming pool is still very popular in the summer! It truly is a joy to see the family growing.

The fourth generation: Teddy, Sebastian, Florence and Joseph

Four generations: Amy, Margaret, Sally and Teddy
*Photograph taken by Guy Lucas of Regent Park Photographics Ltd, in his studio at 19
Clarence Terrace, Regents Park, NW1 4RD*

Epilogue

So, that's the history of me, from both mine and Margaret's perspective. I am now in my seventy ninth year of life and I've never smoked a cigarette nor had a drop of alcohol in all those years. I've led a full and exciting life with some amazing times and indeed some worrying times, but I can say very sincerely that throughout my life I've been the luckiest man I know.

But although I've been very lucky, I've also had to work very hard, and I've always said that 'the harder you work the luckier you become.' I hope this is one of the snippets of wisdom that my children and my grandchildren will take on board. I have tried to guide them as best I can over the years, imparting some small pearls of wisdom whenever I can, although I am aware that they do get a bit fed up with my never-ending advice. I am sure some of it they have heeded and I am equally sure that some of it they have dismissed as quickly as it has been said, but I hope that in writing this book they will be able to realise exactly what is truly important in life; developing strong values, respecting others, and upholding a good work ethic. And to my children and grandchildren I say simply this, "Don't give up on your dreams."

I hope that future generations of my family will appreciate how hard Margaret and I have worked to try and give our children and our grandchildren a good start in life and I hope that they will find this book an inspiration, so that they can go on and make the most of the opportunities that come their way, and ultimately I hope that luck continues to shine down on the Hobbs family.

My final word is this; the two most important decisions you will ever make in your life concern whom you will marry and who you choose to be friends with. I have always said to my children and grandchildren that when choosing friends, particularly at university, you should remember that you become like the people you mix with, therefore you must choose carefully.

My friendship choices and my choice of bride were certainly the most important decisions that I ever made, and thankfully I made the right ones.

Unquestionably, without the support of my wonderful wife we would not have been so successful in life; Margaret... Thank you.